Osage Indian

Customs and Myths

By

Louis F. Burns

THE UNIVERSITY OF ALABAMA PRESS
Tuscaloosa

The University of Alabama Press
Tuscaloosa, Alabama 35487-0380
uapress.ua.edu

First paperback edition 2005
The University of Alabama Press

Cover design: Erin Kirk New

Cataloging-in-Publication data is available from the Library of Congress.
ISBN: 978-0-8173-5181-6 (paper)
ISBN: 978-0-8173-9378-6 (electronic)

To my mother, Bessie Tinker, who

made me proud to be Osage.

TABLE OF CONTENTS

Dedication iii
Preface xi
Part I: Customs 1
Chapter One: The Little Old Men 3
   Qualifications of the Little Old Men 3
   Origin of the Little Old Men 6
   Philosophy of the Little Old Men 8
   Symbolism of the Little Old Men 11
      The Eternal Sun 11
      Order of Presentation 12
      Symbolic Man 12
      The Wa ho pe 13
      The Arrows 13
      Colors of War 14
      Striking the Earth 15
      Haircuts 16
      Left and Right 20
      Prayer Eagles 20
      Symbolic Birth 21
      Seizing Firewood 21
   Sayings, Thoughts, and Allegory of the Little Old Men . . . 22
      Allegory of the Sky 22
      The Milky Way 23
      Door to the Future 24
      The Path of Life 24
      The Bends in the River of Life 24
      Sayings 24
Chapter Two: Government 27
   Introduction 27
   Legendary History of Organization 29
   Final Military Government 31
   Creation of the Civil Government 32
   Separation of Civil and Military Power 35
   Executive Limitation 36

Judiciary Powers. 36
The Military and the White Man. 36
Chapter Three: Religion. 39
Introduction 39
Overview 41
   Buffalo Bull Order 41
   The Seven Songs 41
   The Six Songs 42
   Skins 43
The Seven Songs 43
   Ceremony of Blowing on the Skins. 43
   Shaping the Moccasins .44
   Adornment 47
   The Footstep Prayer 48
   Song of Opening the Shrine 48
   Standing at His Fireplace. 49
   Early Morning Song 49
   Wolf Songs 50
   Isolated Song of the Hawk. 50
   Song of Taking the Rattle. 51
   Rite of Vigil 52
   Making the Bow. 53
   Spirit Songs. 53
   Midday Sun Songs. 54
   Afternoon Songs. 55
   Fish-Turtle Song 55
   Wolf Songs 55
   Seizing the Wa to pa. .56
   Dream Prayer. 56
   Wailing Songs 56
   Song of the Wa to pa .57
   Crow Songs. 57
   Buffalo Songs 58
The Six Songs. 59
   Stand-by of Men, Buffalo Songs 59
   Deer Song. 59

Black Bear Song. 59
The Rush for Charcoal 60
Water Songs 60
Star Songs 61
The Great Evening Songs 61
Little Evening Songs 62
Snake Songs 62
The Great Rain Songs 63
The Little Rain Songs 63
Releasing the Arrows Song 64
Songs of Making One Strike the Other 64
Victory Song. 65
Song of Closing the Ceremony 65
Uses of the Rite of Vigil 65
Penalities 66
Sending of Will Power. 67
Sham War 67
Introduction. 67
Name Taking 68
Charcoal Fight 69
The Attack 70
Conclusion 71
Chapter Four: Marriage, Child Naming-Adoption,
        and Education 73
Marriage. 73
Introduction. 73
Me shin (New Grown) 75
O me ho (Those Who Have Married Before). 77
Ka shon le Me gro ka (Those Who Have Married
        Recklessly) 78
Cultural Conflicts in Marriage. 79
Child Naming and Adoption 80
Child Naming. 80
Introduction 80
Child Naming Ceremony 81
Adoption 85

Introduction 85
Adoption Ceremony 85
Comments 87
Education. 88
Introduction. 88
Crow Butte 89
The Hunter 90
Parents. 92
Osage Mothers 93
Chapter Five: Hunting, Planting, and Gathering 97
Hunting 97
Introduction. 97
Buffalo Trails 98
The Grand Buffalo Hunt .101
Processing Hides and Meat 104
The Winter Hunt 107
Planting 108
Introduction. 108
Processing, Storage, and Use. 109
Corn Ceremonies 111
Gathering. 112
Introduction. 112
Minerals 112
Vegetative Material 114
Medicinal Herbs 115
Firewood 117
Wild Food Plants 118
Cookery. 121
Chapter Six: War 125
Introduction 125
Organization of a War Party 126
The Symbolic Man. 128
War Paint 129
Strategies and Tactics 129
Valor Adornments 132
War Honors. 136

The Seven War Honors 136
The Six War Honors...........................138
Wa shin Le le Ke non 139
Chapter Seven: Mourning 143
  Introduction 143
  Origin of Mourning War 143
  Mourning Ceremony for Fallen Warriors............144
  Adornment for Burial...........................146
  Changes 147
  Burial 147
  Looting Graves 148
Chapter Eight: General Customs 151
  Dress 151
  Curtesies 153
  Types of Communication 154
    Oral Language 154
    Body Language............................154
    Finger Talk...............................155
    Dancing and Dramaturgy 155
    Pictorial Art 155
  Fire Building 168
  Hair Custom 170
  Respect Toward Relatives........................170
  Parfleches................................170
Part Two: Myths 175
Chapter Nine: Genesis Myths........................177
  Introduction 177
  Different Versions...........................178
  Genesis Myth (Panther Clan Version) 179
  Genesis Myth (Black Bear Version) 183
  Genesis Myth (Elder Tsi shu Version).............185
  Genesis Myth (Wearers of Symbolic Locks Version) .187
  Genesis Myth (Tsi shu Peacemaker Version) 191
Chapter Ten: General Myths 195
  Animal Myths...............................195
    Buffalo 195

Black Bear.................................196
Beaver 197
Another Beaver Myth 197
Dog 198
Eagles 198
Avengers 199
The Owl and Hawk.........................200
Hawk Wa ho pe............................201
Animals in Great Bodies of Water 202
Large Animals 202
Name Myths 203
Star Names...............................203
Sky and Earth Names (Black Bear and
    Panther Clans)........................204
Earth Names (Black Bear and Panther People)...205
Personal Names (Buffalo Bull People)..........206
Tsi shu Personal Names......................206
Symbolic Knives 207
Special Myths 207
Upper Worlds.............................207
Tribal Organization 208
Formation of the Tribe 208
Hun ka..................................211
The Search for Isolated Earth 212
Child's Robe..............................213
Corn Planting 214
Striking the Earth..........................214
Peace Gods and Goddesses..................215
Siren....................................216
Mystic Arrows 217
Clouds 217
The Dreams 217

LIST OF MAPS, CHARTS AND ILLUSTRATIONS

Map of Osage Territory xii
Fig.   1.   Haircut of the Last in the Hun ka Order Clan . .16
Fig.   2.   Haircut of the Tsi shu Peacemaker Clan 17
Fig.   3.   Haircut of Tails Worn on the Head Clan 18
Fig.   4.   Haircut of the Men of Mystery Clan 18
Fig.   5.   Haircut of the Buffalo Bull Clan 19
Fig.   6.   Chart of Osage Tribal Organization 28
Fig.   7.   A Prompter Adorned for Ceremonies 46
Fig.   8.   Child's Robe 84
Fig.   9.   An Arrowshaft Polishing Block 114
Fig.   10.   A Tattooed Osage Man .134
Fig.   11.   A Tattooed Osage Woman. 135
Fig.   12.   Ho e ka Variations. 159
Fig.   13.   Diamond Variations. 159
Fig.   14.   Morning Star. 159
Fig.   15.   Striking the Earth. 159
Fig.   16.   Osage Spider. 159
Fig.   17.   Design from a Large Parfleche 160
Fig.   18.   Design from a Small Parfleche 161
Fig.   19.   Ribbonwork Designs 162
Fig.   20.   Ribbonwork Design 163
Fig.   21.   Beadwork Rosette from a Moccasin 163
Fig.   22.   Beadwork Design from a Moccasin 163
Fig.   23.   Beadwork Head Band from an Osage Bonnet . .164
Fig.   24.   Design from a Beaded Vest 164
Fig.   25.   Beaded Design from a Girl's Moccasin 164
Fig.   26.   Beaded Design of the Morning Star 165
Fig.   27.   Beaded Design of the Evening Star. 165
Fig.   28.   Beaded Design of the "Tree of Life" 165
Fig.   29.   Beaded Design of the Four Upper Worlds
                Resting on the Red Oak 165
Fig.   30.   Friction Fire Starting Components 168

Preface

The Osage are a Siouan people who occupied the central portion of the United States. They were the parent tribe of the Dhegiha Sioux. Their splinter tribes were the Omaha, Ponca, Kansas, and Quapaw. In all, there were eleven Siouan groups identified as Siouan people. The Dakota-Asiniboin is the group most commonly called Sioux. Chewere Sioux were the Iowa, Otoe, and Missouri tribes. These were neighboring tribes to the Osage. In fact, half of the surviving Missouris joined the Osages in 1812. The other half joined their kindred tribe, the Otoes in Iowa. Other Siouan groups were the Winnebago, Mandan, Hidatsa, Biloxi, Monakan, Catawba, Sara, and Pedee. The last two groups named are now extinct. [1]

Language comparisons with the Catawba clearly indicate the Siouan peoples of the Plains migrated from the Atlantic Coastal Region of the United States. [2] The Chesapeake Bay area was probably the prehistoric homeland of the Dhegiha Sioux. They evidently crossed the Potomac Gap and followed the Ohio River to the Mississippi River. The Quapaw or Down River People splintered off the parent group at this time and settled near the mouth of the Arkansas River. However, they continued to maintain amiable relationships with the parent group. Shortly after the original group crossed the Mississippi River, the Omaha and Ponca splintered off. These were called the Up River People. The Omaha settled on the bluff which gave them their name. O ma ha means People Who Live on the Bluff. Gradually, the Ponca followed the Platte River into the Southern Black Hills. [3]

[1] W.J. McGee, "The Siouan Indians," *Smithsonian Institution, BAE, 15th Annual Report,* (Government Printing Office: Washington, 1897), pp. 160-165.

[2] *Ibid.,* p. 159.

[3] The Osages called the Platte River, Ne bra scah or Flat Water White, because of the white reflection of the sun on the shallow braids of water.

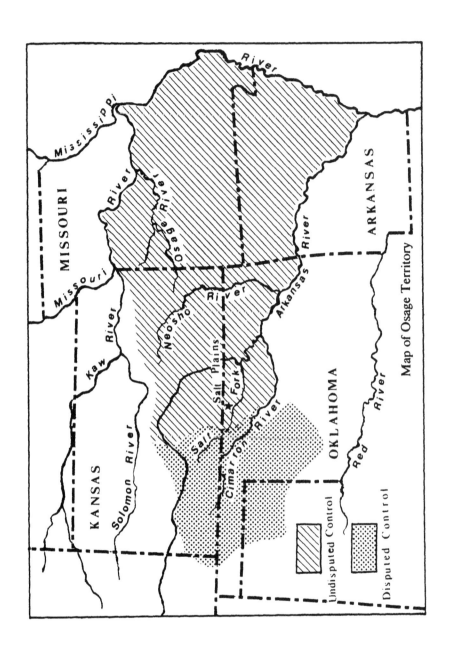

Map of Osage Territory

Undisputed Control

Disputed Control

MISSOURI

KANSAS

ARKANSAS

OKLAHOMA

Mississippi

Missouri River

Kaw River

Solomon River

Osage River

Neosho River

Arkansas River

Salt Plains

Salt Fork

Cimarron River

Red River

River

When the remaining Dhegiha came to the Osage River, the Kon za or Kansas splintered off and settled on the Kansas River. In general, the Osage and Kansas enjoyed friendly relationships, but the Kansas refused to aid the Osage against the Sac and Fox, as a result the Osage always called them Kaw or Coward. The parent group was called Ne U Kon scah or People of the Middle Waters. However, they are better known as Osage.

A partial split occurred when the Osages migrated up the Osage River. Six bands of the Little Osages settled between Glasgow and Malta Bend, Missouri. However, they continued to share the same gentile organization, customs, defence, and the hunt. Another partial split came shortly after 1800 when the Pomme Terre River bands split from the Vernon County, Missouri bands and moved to the Verdigris-Grand River in Oklahoma. This, too, was not a complete separation for marriage and ceremony sharing was still practiced in common.

In general, Osage territory was bounded on the north by the Missouri River and the divide between the Kansas River watershed and the Neosho River watershed in Kansas. The Mississippi River formed the eastern boundary and the Arkansas River was the southern boundary. While the Osages held undisputed control as far as the western edge of the Salt Plains, they also had disputed control as far west as the Colorado line.

This is the background in which Osage customs and myths existed. Their customs and myths show a strong relationship to the customs and myths of other Siouan peoples. In many instances, they show similiarities to their Pawnee, Kiowa, Wichita, Comanche, Apache, and Cheyenne enemies on the Plains. In those closing days of the traditional ways, before the last of the Southern Buffalo Herd perished, these were the tribes who extended their hands in friendship. They did not understand the disorderly world of the white man, but they understood each other.

We must explain that orderliness to the Indian mind meant to live as a part of the environment. To live in conflict with the environment was disorderly since it was artificial and not natural.

The tearing of the Sacred Earth with plows; the wanton disregard for animal life; and seizure of land by individual owners were all horrible violations of the natural order to the Indian mind. Because of the difficulties in exchanging thoughts between the cultures, these feelings of the Osage sometimes caused conflicts between the Osages and the settlers.

It is sometimes difficult to convey in English the true meaning of many Osage words and expressions. We have tried to keep the Osage words to a minimum and to give their approximate meanings in English. Hopefully, a reader will not experience any difficulty in understanding the Osage expressions. Explanatory footnotes were added in many places to clarify these expressions. An effort was made to write so the young and the old; the layman and the scholar; the interested and the curious could find the Osages a worthy subject to read about.

A suggestion to the reader may be worth considering. The Osage culture was different than the cultures of Western Civilization. Therefore, the reader should literally place his or her mind in neutral. This is especially difficult to do because there are many things the cultures have in common. The problem comes when an alien practice or thought pattern appears. It is natural for humans to measure the strange against the yardstick of the familiar. Yet, when we do this we are lifting the practice or thought out of context. Imagine how an Osage of 1750 would interpret an American football game of today. To him, it would have seemed to be some kind of religious ceremony. This would be caused by measuring a football game by an Indian's religion centered cultural yardstick. In its own context, a football game could never be mistaken for a religious ceremony.

Osage myths differ greatly from the myths of Western Civilization. The most obvious difference is the absence of individual names. Osage myths do not use names of individuals. Younger brother, elder brother, the messenger, a man, or the name of a clan such as Radiant Star are used in lieu of a personal name. Heroic feats of individuals are also absent. Partly, this is because the group such as clan, subdivision, division, or tribe took precedence over the individual in Osage life.

One must also be aware of how these customs and myths were transmitted from one generation to the next. The Osage did not have a written language. Therefore, everything had to be committed to memory. Of necessity, only those things deemed vital were preserved. These in turn were highly stylized so as to retain only the basic ideas. The Osage language does not have the extensive vocabulary of the English language. Much of the thought comes from the actions rather than from the words. In addition, those who memorized these myths and customs were also taught back-grounds in the form of legends. These were seldom recorded or remembered because they had no religious function.

In a religion centered society such as the Osage culture, religion permeates every custom and act in the life of the people. For this reason, it is impossible to say of any custom, institution, or act, "This is an act of government and that is a matter of religion." We have divided the book into two parts. Part One deals with customs and Part Two deals with myths, but a strong current of religion flows through both parts.

The five basic institutions of the Osage culture were: The Society of Little Old Men; Government; Religion; The Family; and Education. We have combined The Family and Education in one chapter. The other institutions are dealt with in single chapters. Next, the basic needs are discussed in a single chapter. What is called the "higher needs" is so evident in other chapters, that we did not include them as a separate topic. War could easily be considered as an institution among the Osage, however, we did not class it as an institution. Mourning and death are a common experience in all cultures, but because of what they reveal about the Osage they were given a chapter. As so often happens, a variety of customs defy classification, yet they give valuable insights to the reader. With this in mind, we included a General Customs chapter.

We have divided the second part into two chapters. The first chapter has an introduction to Osage myths and the genesis or creation myths. Finally, the last chapter is a collection of general myths with some loose classification. These are Animal Myths, Special Myths, and Name Myths.

It would be a very selfish act if we did not pay tribute to Dr. Francis La Flesche for recording Osage information. However, a greater tribute must be given to those wonderful, foresighted, Little Old Men who left for their descendants, their memories of the rites, ceremonies, legends, and myths. We hope these customs and myths recreate for the reader the mysterious, robust world of the Osages.

PART

I

CUSTOMS

CHAPTER I

Nun ho Shin ka

The Little Old Men

Qualifications of the Little Old Men

All Osage activities were influenced by an organization called Nun ho Shin ka or Little Old Men. At times, these men are called the Ancient Men and the Old Ones. The name, Little Old Men is somewhat deceptive. Both little and old are used, in this sense, as terms of respect and humility. They merited respect for their humility before the Sovereign Being of the Universe.

None of the Little Old Men were ordinary men, all were exceptional persons. Requirements for initiation into this unusual organization assured excellence in its membership. Not only were they outstanding warriors, but they were also mentally and ethically superior persons.[1] Ancient Greek philosophers idealized the "authentic man." This thought is stressed in the story of Demosthenes wandering the streets of Athens at night, carrying a lantern. When asked why he was doing this, his reply is misquoted as: "I am searching for an honest man." The more accurate quote would be: "I am searching for an authentic man." Demosthenes would have come closer to finding his ideal in the Osage villages than in Athens.

To appreciate the "authenticity" of the Little Old Men one must be aware of what was required of a candidate. There are seven war rites and nearly as many peace rites. Each of the

---

[1] J. Owen Dorsey, "Osage Traditions," *Smithsonian Institution, BAE, 6th Annual Report,* (Government Printing Office: Washington, 1888), p. 377.

twenty-four clans had their own versions of these rites. To be initiated into each of the war and peace rites a collection of gifts and supplies for feasts had to be accumulated. Up to seven years were allowed to accomplish this. Once set aside for the initiation, the gifts and supplies could not be used for any other purpose. This feat alone demonstrated an extraordinary energy and strong moral fiber. It was no small task to seek out the necessary ceremonial animals and slay them for their skins, armed only with bow and arrows. During the years of accumulating the gifts and stores, hunger often visited the candidate. He sat amid the store of ceremonial foodstuff, yet would not touch a single morsel though his body cried for food. His family hungered with him but the ceremonial stores were not touched.[2] Another requirement also illustrates strong ethical and moral character.

A candidate must have been named in the tribal child-naming ceremony and raised under the rules prescribed by custom. He must have attained the title of "honorable man," or as they were more commonly called "good man," by living his life according to the ideals of the tribe. His marriage must have been arranged according to the strict code of the tribe. In addition, he must have distinguished himself by protecting the women in the fields and the village. A lifetime of generosity was also required. Normally, this meant that he had given away everything he owned at least three times. From earliest childhood, the Little Old Men watched the young men for signs of devotion to tribal ceremonies and intelligence. Only the devout and intelligent were admitted to candidacy in the organization.[3]

Intelligence was a necessity in the organization. All of the accumulated wisdom of Osage existence depended on the Little

[2] Francis La Flesche, "The Osage Tribe: The Rite of Vigil," *Smithsonian Institution, BAE, 39th Annual Report*, (Government Printing Office: Washington, 1925), p. 44.

[3] Francis La Flesche, "The Osage Tribe: Rite of the Wa Xo' Be," *Smithsonian Institution, BAE, 45th Annual Report*, (U.S. Government Printing Office: Washington, 1930), pp. 532-534.

Old Men for transmission from one generation to the next. In a sense, the Little Old Men were a living library. The war and peace ceremonies would require many volumes of printed pages if put into print.[4] This would include the We ke a s and songs of the ceremonies and the dramatic actions which help explain the ceremonies. Not included would be the non-ceremonial legends which explain much about the ceremonies. All of this had to be learned and retained by a candidate. Without a written language this was a staggering mental feat. The only aid to the mind was a counting stick and a bundle of wands. These were called Shon ha wa shu, literally, Wands to Place Upon.

A counting stick was usually about eighteen inches long and slightly over an inch wide. Thin grooves were cut across the width. Some of the grooves were in groups and others stood alone, depending on how the song or songs were presented in the ceremonies. Each groove represented a song. The front side of the stick represented Part One of the ceremony and the reverse side Part Two. When used, the grooves were counted from the bottom to the top, starting with the front side. The thumbnail was inserted into a groove when a song was started and it was not removed until it was time to start the next song. When the top groove, or last song of Part One was finished, the stick was turned end-for-end which brought the reverse side facing the holder. Then the thumbnail was inserted in the bottom groove, which represented the first song in Part Two of the ceremony. The Catholic Rosary is a similar device except it uses beads to keep track of repetitious prayers while the ceremonial Osage songs were varied. Each groove represented a wooden wand as well as a ceremonial song.

Wooden wands about the size of an arrow shaft were also used in counting. A bundle of these wands may be as large as seventy-five sticks. They were primarily used in teaching a

[4] La Flesche, *39th Ann. Rpt., op. cit.,* pp. 37-38.

[5] Francis La Flesche, "War Ceremony and Peace Ceremony of the Osage Indians," *Smithsonian Institution, BAE, Bulletin 101,* (U.S. Government Printing Office: Washington, 1939), pp. 213-216.

candidate the names of the sets of songs and how many songs were in each set. At times the wands were also used to keep track of the songs as they were sung during an actual ceremony. When stored, these wands were made into a bundle and bound at each end and the middle. While counting sticks and wands do help cue the memory, they cannot supply the intelligence to use them properly.[6] We have been stressing their intelligence but the Little Old Men were also great warriors.

Most of the Ancient Men could count all thirteen war honors among their achievements. Among these war honors were leadership of both grand and small war parties. The highest war honors were those which involved protection of the women and village. Honors won in offensive warfare ranked lower than honors won in defensive warfare. All of the Old Ones held leadership and defensive honors.[7] We find in the Little Old Men, the ancient Greek concept of mental and physical development as well as the great ethical integrity necessary to attain the title of authentic men. We have tried to give a hint about the qualifications of the Ancient Men, because of their importance in the Osage culture. They were truly warriors, scholars, statesmen, and priests. To more fully comprehend the significance of this distinguished body of humans, it is necessary to explore their origin.

Origin of the Little Old Men

For an undetermined span of time the Osage had no rules for defense or living. This condition was called Ka ne la, Without Order.[8] They were groups of people who were living together for

---

[6] *Loc. cit.*

[7] La Flesche, *39th Ann. Rpt., op. cit.,* pp. 67-68.

[8] Francis La Flesche, "The Osage Tribe: Two Versions of the Child-Naming Rite," *Smithsonian Institution, BAE, 43rd Annual Report,* (U.S. Government Printing Office: Washington, 1928), pp. 29-30.

mutual protection. In time, a group of men formed the habit of meeting and discussing a variety of topics. Usually they discussed problems which beset their people, however, they also discussed the meaning of things they observed in the world around them. This group of men gradually acquired the title of Little Old Men. The house where they met came to be called Nun ho Shin ka Wa le Tsa, or House of the Little Old Men. Nearly every morning the Ancient Men met in this house. Although some of these meetings were official, they were more often informal. Solutions were found for problems that were harmful. Any thing that generated friendliness and kindness among the people was encouraged by the men in the sacred house.

No specific house was built and maintained by the Old Ones for the meetings. It was customary for the Little Old Men to select the lodge of a man who was honored and respected by the people. This house was not required to be from any special clan, but the owner was required to be a Little Old Man. He was given the title of, Keeper of the Little Old Men. This title had two meanings: (1) it meant his home sheltered the Ancient Men when they sat in deliberation; and (2) it meant he was the presiding officer of the Little Old Men when they were in deliberation or in the ceremonies. To be selected for this honor was the highest possible tribute to a home owner.[9]

Although the names Little Old Men and Ancient Men are masculine, a few women were almost always members of the society. These women were widows of men who had been members. In an honorable marriage, a husband and wife were considered to be a single entity. Thus, the widow was the living part of the deceased member. However, the widow must apply for membership and approval of the society before being initiated into the organization. She was represented by a Little Old Man of her husband's clan in this application. The initiation We ke a or ceremony is also of her husband's clan. All references to killing is omitted from the ceremony for women are the channel through

---

[9] La Flesche, *Bull. 101, op. cit.,* pp. 3-4.

which all human life must pass and the person who feeds and cares for the helpless new life.[10]

Contrary to the popular American opinion of the treatment of Indian women, the Osages respected and honored their women. Men and women alike had a hard life. Yet, it is provable that Osage women reached old age in far greater numbers than Osage men.[11] This is a primary reason for a man having multiple wives. Actually few men were killed in warfare, most died as a result of the rigors of the hunt and war. Osage women were aware of this and so pampered their men. This view of the Little Old Men toward women was a part of their philosophy. While their philosophy was not as systemized as the idealism of the ancient Greeks, nevertheless it had some surprising facets.

Philosophy of the Little Old Men

The Ancient Men sought the meaning of what they were able to observe. As with all men, the heavenly bodies, and the cycles of day and night puzzled them. They discussed these things among themselves over a long period of time. Slowly, they reached some conclusions about the universe. The order and regularity in all they observed suggested to them the presence of some controlling force. The rising of the sun, its passage across the heavens, and its disappearance over and over, lifetime after lifetime was too significant to pass unnoticed. Coming of darkness with the vastness of the sky covered with the heavenly bodies also followed orderly behavior. Death of plants in the winter and the rebirth that came in the spring also impressed the Ancient Men. All of these observations convinced the Little Old Men that an intelligent force existed in the universe which they called Wa kon ta.[12]

[10] La Flesche, *39th Ann. Rpt., op. cit.,* p. 238.

[11] Louis F. Burns, *The Osage Annuity Rolls of 1878, First Roll,* (Ciga Press: Fallbrook, CA, 1980), p. 3.

[12] La Flesche, *43rd Ann. Rpt., op. cit.*

8

To these ancient sages, this Mysterious Being created the sun, the moon, the stars and the earth. Then He brought life in all its many forms from the darkness into the life sustaining daylight. They also concluded that this Mysterious Force resided in the heavenly bodies and on the earth.[13] The regularity in the universe concept was applied to the Osage people.

Life was considered to be a continuing thing like the movements of the sun. It rises each morning from the unseen to the seen. To the Ancient Men human life was beauty and joy, like the sunrise, so it was desirable to preserve life to provide continuity. Along with this they saw the tragedies and sorrows of life. Times of war were comparable to a plunge into the mysterious oblivion of death. After the conflict, the living emerge from darkness and returns to the light of day.[14]

The Little Old Men were certain that the spirit of the dead had an existence after death. In the Wa non ha Wa lo or Spirit Songs, the singer mentions his visits to the land of spirits. He also sings that his footprints are already upon the spirit path, even though he lives. This is to say, each day we live we draw closer to the spirit land. It is interesting to note that the Ancient Men had the Wind clan conduct the Spirit Ceremonies. How poetic it is, that they heard the voices of the dead in the wind sounds. Like sailors at sea, the Osages did not like for anyone to whistle. Both Osages and sailors listened to the voice of the winds. There were other parallels between the thoughts of the Little Old Men and Western Civilization.[15]

In the Supplication Songs is a reference to the transference of will. The Osages called for this power when they faced danger. In practice, it was similar to the Catholic concept of the Mass, although it differed in detail. Transference of will as conceived by the Ancient Men, placed the unity of the entire tribe behind a

[13] La Flesche, *45th Ann. Rpt., op. cit.,* p. 569.

[14] *Ibid.,* p. 570.

[15] *Ibid.,* pp. 596-597.

warrior in combat. Each tribal member at daily intervals prayed to Wa kon ta to give their warriors the necessary traits to win. This was a conscious effort to transfer by thought, the necessary power to win a victory.[16]

Two other mental exercises of the Little Old Men are worth noting. Synthesizing as a mental process was clearly used by the Ancient Men. That is, new ideas were generated by combining existing ideas in different ways. This is the mental ladder by which all mankind has climbed from the caves to higher levels of civilization. Another mental tool used by the Little Old Men was what they called, "exploring with the mind." This was a mental process akin to deductive and inductive reasoning. The presence of this "exploring with the mind," shows the Ancient Men were on the threshold of civilization.

We do not know of any Western Civilization parallel to the Osage concept of Ho e ka which is common to other Siouan people. This concept is well stated in the Ho e ka Ke pa sha Wa lo or Songs of Walking Over the Earth. Ho e ka is a ceremonial name for the earth, however, it also means a snare or trap. The Little Ones envisioned the earth as a trap into which all life falls. Life is ensnared here on earth and it cannot escape except by death. This comes from the basic concept that all material forms of life come from the combined power of the sky and earth. Ke pa sha means to travel over the earth.[17] It also carries the connotation that the earth is in the custodial care of living humans. This is comparable to a farmer walking over his fields and thinking about their care. The Ancient Men sum up the thought of creating life in this statement: "The sky is the father and the earth is the mother of all living things."

The Ho e ka design on the cover shows the snare as an open-ended rectangle with four short lines inside the rectangle. These short lines represent the four winds, which give the breath of life to the living and carry the voices of the dead as they leave the open

[16] La Flesche, *39th Ann. Rpt., op. cit.,* p. 111.

[17] *Ibid.,* p. 362.

10

end of the snare. This version of the Ho e ka is often used in beadwork and ribbonwork. However, some very old work have only two short lines in the trap. According to Osage mythology, the winds originally blew in only two directions. It blew from the north and then turned and blew from the south. In other designs this is considered as a single wind so only one wind line is drawn. Another variation is to show only three wind lines, the reason being that the south wind was considered to be an evil wind. These symbols may be found in the designs of almost all the Siouan groups.

The thoughts of the Little Old Men were transmitted in ritual form and they were guarded against desecration by teaching them only to pupils who displayed a proper spirit of reverence for things sacred.[18] We have only touched on a few of the concepts of the Ancient Men. Many others will emerge as we progress through this book. However, to help the reader enrich his or her comprehension we feel a brief discussion of symbols is advisable. Many of the rituals were symbolic so as to protect them from the uninitiated. Metaphors and archaic words were also used to hide the true meanings. When the Ancient Men taught these rituals to a candidate, they also taught the pupil the true meaning hidden by these safeguards.[19] With this in mind, let us now turn to some of the symbols.

Symbolism of the Little Old Men

The Eternal Sun

Gorgets made from the shell of a fresh-water mussel symbolized two things. First, it symbolized a concept of the Ancient Men, that the sun was the only thing in the universe that endures forever. Second, it is a symbol of a long life.[20]

[18] La Flesche, *45th Ann. Rpt., op. cit.,* p. 532. ·

[19] *Loc. cit.*

[20] *Ibid.,* p. 555.

Order of Presentation

In the Early Morning Songs, the sun is presented in the human form. This is to stress the coming of humans from the invisible to the visible world. The order of presentation is as follows: First, the head appears, followed by the arms, body, legs, and finally the feet. When the human body or any other body is presented in this order, in a ceremony, it is symbolic of birth. If the reverse order is followed, that is if the feet are first, this represents the growth of man and his life's journey from infancy to old age.[21]

Symbolic Man

When designing the rites intended to preserve tribal unity, the Ancient Men gave thought to the internal and external dangers to the tribe. They were determined that the two grand divisions must meet these dangers with one mind and one action. To symbolize this unity of thought and action they created a symbolic man. The symbolic man's body was made of the two grand divisions. When at peace the symbolic man faced the east, the direction of life. This placed the left side of the symbolic man on the Tsi shu or Sky side of the tribal circle. The symbolic man's right side would be on the Hun ka or Earth side of the circle. When the tribe prepared for war the symbolic man turned and faced the west, the direction of death. This turning of the symbolic man to the west caused a reversing of the normal order of the tribal circle. The Tsi shu were still on the left but they were now on the south side of the circle and the Hun ka were on the north side. When the symbolic man faced east he stood for the peace side of the tribal organization; when he faced the west he stood for the war side.[22]

[21]*Ibid.*, pp. 567-568.

[22]*Ibid.*, pp. 549-550.

The Wa ho pe

The Wa ho pe was a shrine. There were two major Wa ho pe s. One was very ancient and was called the Great Shrine; the other was the Hawk Shrine or Portable Shrine. The Wa ho pe Gra to or Hawk Shrine was carried by the eight commanders of a war party. Most Americans describe this shrine as a bag filled with all manner of disgusting things or simply as a medicine bag.

Wa ho pe s contained a dried hawk in three bags or covers. The Ancient Men gave the hawk emblem, child of the sun and moon, a great deal of symbolism. They gave to the coverings of the Wa ho pe the symbols of their concepts of Wa kon ta being in the sky and earth. In a sense, the covering of the Wa ho pe is a record of their concepts.

The first cover, on the outside, was a cover of woven buffalo hair; next, in the middle, was a deerskin cover; and finally the inner cover which was made of woven rushes. This third cover or sack was decorated with symbols of sky and earth. The space within the inner sack is symbolic of the space between the sky and the earth. This space is also symbolic of the Ho e ka concept. The ceremonial act of removing the hawk was symbolic of birth and the continuous progressive flow of life.[23]

The Arrows

The Songs of Releasing the Arrows with their symbolism and dramatic action are prayers. They are indications of a desire for divine aid to continue tribal existence. In addition, they are prayers to Wa kon ta to give to the individual an endless line of descent. One arrow is red to represent day and the other is black to represent night. The facing side of the ceremonial bow is red and the reverse side is black. This dramatic prayer is directed to Wa kon ta through his home, night and day. Both arrows are shot

[23]*Ibid.*, pp. 530-531.

toward the west so they may chase forever the night and day that mark the span of time for all life.[24]

Colors of War

Charcoal, preferably made of redbud but sometimes made of willow, was a symbol of merciless warfare. Black was the symbol of the all-consuming wildfire that destroyed everything in its path. It was a symbol of death. The black bear was also a symbol of fire because of the light that sometimes flashed from its chest. Panther eyes flash fire in the dark, thus, it too was a fire symbol. Both the Black Bear clan and its kindred Panther clan were leading war clans. White swans were prized as a war symbol because of its black bill and feet, but most of all for their strength and endurance.[25]

When the Osage warriors wore charcoal over the entire face it meant a no quarter fight against enemy men, women, and children. If the warrior wore charcoal on the upper face and yellow on the lower face he was engaged in "bluff war." This type of warfare involved "baiting" an enemy with insults. These insults were delivered with "finger talk" which is commonly called sign language. This was used because of the distance between the aggressive and defensive parties. The verbal language does not have any vile words; "finger talk" had a full range of expression. "Bluff war" was usually a war of warriors and did not involve women, children, and the elderly.

If a warrior blackened his entire face and added two vertical yellow stripes to each cheek and wore a wavy black line up the outside of each leg, he was seeking a scalp. These were the markings used by a mourning war party who sought to kill and enemy to travel the path to spirit land with a deceased Osage.[26]

[24] La Flesche, *39th Ann. Rpt., op. cit.*, p. 364; La Flesche, *45th Ann. Rpt., op. cit.*, p. 675.

[25] La Flesche, *39th Ann. Rpt., op. cit.*, p. 327.

[26] *Ibid.*, p. 73.

14

Striking the Earth

Striking the earth enacts the belief that through the interaction of sky and earth, life emerges in its physical form. It is also symbolic of the tribal gentile organization and unity.

During the ceremony the earthen floor of the House of Mysteries is struck with a war club. Next a straight line is drawn from the dent to the west with the war club. This is followed by drawing a wavy line from the dent to the north. Again a straight line is drawn, this time it is drawn from the dent to the east. Finally another wavy line is drawn, but it is drawn from the dent to the south.

The dent represents the midday sun. The straight lines represent the daily path of the sun. Both wavy lines represent the life giving warmth of the sun's rays. When drawn vertically, these lines represent the four winds. On the human torso the wavy lines are placed on the sides and the straight lines on the front and back.[27]

The four winds are sometimes depicted ceremonially. To do this, the arms are raised then brought down quickly. First, the hands describe a wavy line which represents the violence and destruction of the north wind. Second, the hands describe a straight line which represents the gentle, life-giving touch of the east wind. Third, the hands describe a wavy line which represents hot south winds which destroy plants. Fourth, the hands describe a straight line which represents the refreshing winds and rains of the west wind.[28]

At times wavy grooves are observed on arrow shafts. One suggestion is that the arrow will bring life giving food to the user if it has these marks. Another suggestion is that it is an aid to help the arrow penetrate its target. A final suggestion is that it is done to keep the arrow from warping.

[27]*Ibid.*, pp. 359-361.

[28]*Loc. cit.*

Haircuts

Each of the twenty-four Osage clans had a symbolic haircut worn by their children. Both boys and girls wore these clan hair styles until they reached the age of ten years. Adult males wore a roach from front to back down the center of the head. Women wore their hair long with a part down the middle. On some occasions this part was colored red to represent the sun's path. Unmarried women often wore their hair in front of the shoulders. Married women kept their hair behind the shoulders. The symbolic haircuts of the children were meant as a prayer to Wa kon ta to grant a long life to the child.[29]

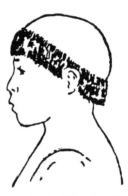

Fig. 1.   Haircut of the Last in the Hun ka Order Clan
(Drawn from an illustration in Smithsonian, BAE, 43rd Annual Report.)

The haircut illustrated in Fig. 1, represented the Little Rock of the Marsh, which was also called the Gentle Rock because it was a special symbol of peace and happiness to the Last in the Hun ka Order clan. A fringe of hair was left around the bare crown. This fringe copied the moss which clung to the Gentle Rock near the water line. The bare crown represented the bare dome of the rock.[30]

[29]Louis F. Burns, "Cultural Heritage," *Osage News,* Nov., 1983, (United Osages Association of Southern California: Fallbrook, CA), pp. 7-8.

[30]*Loc. cit.*

Fig. 2.   Haircut of the Tsi shu Peacemaker Clan
(Drawn from an illustration in Smithsonian, B.A.E, 43rd Annual Report.)

In the origin myth of the Tsi shu, the last two eagles tried to land in the red oak with the other eagles. However, the tree was overburdened with eagles, so one alit in an elder tree and the other alit amid cone flowers. The Osage call the elder tree Ba po; its wood is used for the stem of ceremonial pipes. Cone flowers are called Kla Se Shin ka or Little Yellow Flower. This flower is a special symbol of peace to the Last in the Tsi shu Order clan. The haircut representing the Little Yellow Flower left the crown with stubble hair and a circlet of petal shaped hair around the head. (See Fig. 2.) [31]

[31] *Loc. cit.*

17

Fig. 3. Haircut of the Tails Worn on the Head Clan
(Drawn from an illustration in Smithsonian, BAE, 43rd Annual Report.)

The Elder Tsi shu clan used a hair pattern called Sin tse ah gra or Tails Worn on the Head as shown in Fig. 3. This cut left three locks down the center of the head; each lock was allowed to grow long like a tail. These tails were symbolic of the dog, wolf, and coyote. In addition, the tails represented Shon ka ah ke a ko or Dog that Lies Suspended in the Sky (Canis Major). It is interesting that both the Romans and Osage saw a dog in this constellation.[32]

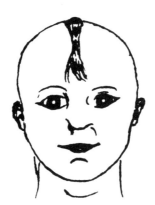

Fig. 4. Haircut of the Men of Mystery Clan

[32]*Loc. cit.*

18

Children's haircuts for the Men of Mystery clan, left only two locks of hair. One lock came forward from the crown to above the mid forehead. Another was at the back of the head near the hairline and centered down the neck. Fig. 4 does not show this back of the head lock. The hawk was a life symbol of the Men of Mystery clan, and the hair style symbolized the courage of their warriors. This haircut depicted the attacking hawk with its wings folded.[33]

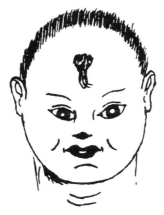

Fig. 5. Haircut of the Buffalo Bull Clan

Another haircut comes from the Buffalo Bull clan. (See Fig. 5.) A little tuft of hair was left over the middle of the forehead, then a fringe ran over the crown from ear to ear. Three tufts were left at the hairline on the back of the head. One of these was centered on the neck and the other two were on the left and right of the rear center tuft. The latter three tufts do not show in the illustration. The front tuft represented the buffalo's beard and the ear to ear fringe represented the hump. Depicting the coming of the buffalo are the three rear tufts. First, the male buffalo came from the darkness into the light. Next came the female buffalo, and then the buffalo calf.[34]

[33]*Loc. cit.*

[34]*Loc. cit.*

Left and Right

The concept of duality and unity of nature was reflected in many ways. Unity of the two grand divisions of the tribe appear in a variety of symbols but the duality is always indicated by the left or right side. In all cases, the Tsi shu is the left side and the Hun ka is the right side.[35] This handedness, left and right, is not confined to the ceremonies. Tsi shu people put the left moccasin on first while members of the Hun ka grand division put the right moccasin on first. If a warrior slept with his back to a tree and inclined his head to the left he was from the Tsi shu. When sleeping prone, the Hun ka slept on the right side. In planting corn, women firmed the soil with the left or right foot depending on the division of their fathers. This same duality, left and right, was observed in dancing; Tsi shu moved to the left; Hun ka moved to the right.

Prayer Eagles

The Osage prayed three times each day, at dawn, midday, and sunset. Three eagles were symbolic of these times of prayer. Prayers at dawn were more sacred than at the other two times. Therefore, the red eagle is symbolic of the dawn prayers. The white eagle is symbolic of the midday prayers and the bald eagle for the sunset prayers. The Tsi shu grand division chief was always taken from the Red Eagle sub-clan of the Tsi shu Peace-maker clan.[36]

Two other eagles called Hu lah and Hun ka appear in the ceremonies. Both of these eagles are golden eagles but Hu lah refers to the adult golden eagle and Hun ka refers to the immature golden eagle.

The Osage thought these were two different species because the tail and wing feathers were the same size but the feathers of the

[35] La Flesche, *39th Ann. Rpt., op. cit.*, p. 115.

[36] *Ibid.*, p. 318.

near mature bird was mottled. The feathers of the mature bird were white with black tips. Hun ka means the Sacred One and the name applied to the earth and immature golden eagle alike. It was the mottled eagle or immature golden eagle that led the people from the fourth upper world to the earth. The Mottled Eagle clan took this name to commemorate this mythological event. Hun ka is held to be the most sacred of all eagles because of its service to the Osages. This eagle was also called the spotless one, which means it was not hated by other birds.

Symbolic Birth

In the Peace Ceremonies the birth of a child is symbolically enacted. The "child" is called Hun ka, the sacred one, like the mottled eagle and the earth. "Birth" is enacted with a ceremonial pipe, commonly called the calumet or peace pipe in the American culture. As the song telling of the birth nears the end, the pipe is held by the mouthpiece between the thumb and fingers. This placed the bowl downward. As the song closes the pipe is allowed to slip from the fingers, but it is caught before touching the ground. Thus, the symbolic birth is depicted. The Hun ka is now born. He is the symbol of peace and innocence for the child is one incapable of holding malice. He also is the symbol of the uninterrupted continuity of the Osage people. When a woman experienced difficulty in child-birth, this dropping of the pipe was sometimes ceremonially performed apart from the rest of the Peace Ceremony.[37]

Seizing Firewood

In a ceremony called Pa tse U ke, literally, contributed to fire, firewood was taken without permission. This was a part of the ceremony of starting a fire to heat ceremonial water. A firebrand was seized from the fireplace of each of four warriors. Each of the

[37] La Flesche, *Bull. 101, op. cit.,* pp. 216-217.

firebrands represented a deer. The act of taking the wood without permission was to remind the warriors that it was their duty to protect the deer from strangers or hostile intruders.[38]

Sayings, Thoughts, and Allegory
of the Little Old Men

As stated earlier, an understanding of symbols enriches comprehension of Osage customs and myths. The examples of symbols already given also reveal some of the devices used by the Ancient Men to teach their concepts. Some sayings, expressions and an allegory are included here to cast more light on the ways of the Little Old Men.

Allegory of the Sky

The ritual called Moh he Le he tse or Sky Controlling, from the Peace Ceremony, contains a beautiful allegory. The ever changing sky was an inspiration to the Ancient Men. They called a clear cloudless day with the blue vault of the sky overhead a peaceful day. It was a symbol of a long life and an endless line of descent. However, in the sky allegory they relate the full range of sky moods from war to peace.[39] ,

The dark clouds that brought first a restless erratic wind which soon became violent as the sounds of thunder became audible, and then lightning and torrents of rain, awed the Ancient Men. They compared these storms to the horrible conflicts between men. Ceremonial references to the winds, the dark clouds, the lightning, and thunder were often used to dramatize evils. While they recognized a necessity for warfare, they stressed that only defensive war was justifiable. War under any pretense always exacted a price from both victor and vanquished. Even the

[38] *Ibid.*, pp. 47-48.

[39] *Ibid.*, pp. 225-229.

victor was left with the dread of retaliation. Whether they were on the hunt or in the fields, this dread would always be with them.[40]

A peaceful sky suggested to the Old Ones that only through peace could they be free of the restrictions of fear. Birds were often used to teach and preserve the concepts of peace. "The bird who sits as though he had been struck with a tinge of red," (Cardinal) is associated with the clouds touched with the red of the rising sun which give a hint of a calm day. The bluejay; the scarlet tanager; the spotted duck; and the "great curlew" are all symbols of desirable days. It is interesting that the white swan was a symbol of both war and peace. If one remember that death is a part of living it is consistent in all respects to combine the two in one symbol. The white swan is a symbol of a sky that is perfect in purity and peace, a cloudless day.[41]

The sky mentioned above is not the physical sky that surrounds us but the sky of man's conduct toward other men. It is a sky which might be overcast with dangerous and destructive clouds of war. The Little Old Men taught that wars could be influenced by men through self-restraint, self-denial and good will. By using these, men could avert the storms of hatred and malice and make the sky of conduct clear and calm.[42]

The Milky Way

After death the spirit travels the spirit path which is the Milky Way. The spirit travels the path until it finds a star of its own. If true love existed between a man and a woman, and one dies, this spirit star will shine brighter for the living lover. A message of comfort will be sent by the winds if the living will listen.[43]

[40] *Loc. cit.*

[41] *Loc. cit.*

[42] *Loc. cit.*

[43] George E. Tinker and C.J. Phillips, editors, "The Osage: Historical Sketch by the Editors," *The Osage Magazine,* June, 1910, pp. 29-37.

Door to the Future

The lodge of the present has a door to the future but it is covered with a flap. We cannot see through the door. Only our thoughts can pass through the flap. We can catch glimpses of the future in our dreams, but only prayers can make them come true.[44]

The Path of Life

The path of life crosses four valleys.[45]

The Bends in the River of Life

Life is a river and we flow with it; we must travel the seven bends in the river of life before we reach days that are calm and peaceful.[46]

Sayings

"The words and the songs arc like birds, they fly away for a time, but they come back again." This was the answer when a Little Old Man was asked how he could remember the words and songs of the ceremonies.[47]

"A father is in duty, bound to instruct his son in the mysteries of life." A comment of respect for his father who taught him the rites, said by a Little Old Man.[48]

[44]*Loc. cit.*

[45]La Flesche, *39th Ann. Rpt., op. cit.,* pp. 253-259.

[46]*Loc. cit.*

[47]La Flesche, *45th Ann. Rpt., op. cit.,* p. 533.

[48]*Loc. cit.*

Bibliography

Burns, Louis F., "Cultural Heritage," *Osage News*, Nov. 1983, United Osages Association of Southern California: Fallbrook, CA.

————, Louis F., *The Osage Annuity Rolls of 1878, First Roll*, Ciga Press: Fallbrook, CA, 1980.

Dorsey, J. Owen, "Osage Traditions," *Smithsonian Institution, Bureau of American Ethnology, Sixth Annual Report*, Government Printing Office: Washington, 1925.

La Flesche, Francis, "The Osage Tribe: The Rite of Vigil," *Smithsonian Institution, Bureau of American Ethnology, Thirty-Ninth Annual Report*, Government Printing Office: Washington, 1925.

————, Francis, "The Osage Tribe: Two Versions of the Child-Naming Rite," *Smithsonian Institution, Bureau of American Ethnology, Forty-Third Annual Report*, U.S. Government Printing Office: Washington, 1928.

————, Francis, "The Osage Tribe: Rite of the Wa Xo' Be," *Smithsonian Institution, Forty-Fifth Annual Report*, U.S. Government Printing Office: Washington, 1930.

————, Francis, "War Ceremony and Peace Ceremony of the Osage Indians," *Smithsonian Institution, Bureau of American Ethnology, Bulletin 101*, U.S. Government Printing Office: Washington, 1939.

Tinker, George E. and C.J. Phillips, editors, "The Osage: Historical Sketch by the Editors," *The Osage Magazine*, June, 1910.

CHAPTER II

Government

Introduction

The Osage governmental organization was actually very different than the forms described by the early writers. For some unexplained reason, most observers of Indian cultures depicted a chief as an absolute monarch of his people. Other observers tempered this by including a war chief and a "medicine man." We are not qualified to say this popular concept of Indian government was true of other tribes or not. Of the Osage people, this version of its government is certainly not true.

Like medieval Europeans, the Osages were theocentric, that is, their religious beliefs were interlaced with all their activities and institutions. Osage religion and government cannot be separated. A few writers thought they observed "witch doctors" among the Osage. This is a strange thought, because the Osage had and still have extreme contempt for fakery. Even an unintentional misrepresentation will bring a storm of abuse upon the originator. The penalty for one who attempted to mumble incantations and cast spells was exile from the village.[1] We mention this because, although the Osages were a deeply religious people, they were also realists and not superstitious fools. Their realism is evident in the revisions they made in their government to meet changing conditions.

---

[1] Francis La Flesche, "The Osage Tribe: The Rite of Vigil," *Smithsonian Institution, BAE, 39th Annual Report,* (Government Printing Office: Washington, 1925), pp. 41-42.

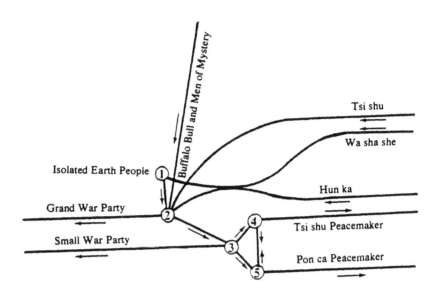

Fig. 6. Chart of Osage Tribal Organization

No. 1 indicates the place occupied by the Isolated Earth people when they were found by the Wa sha she.

No. 2 indicates the "new country" to which the Wa sha she and isolated Earth people moved. Here they were joined by the Hun ka and Tsi shu. These four groups created the Grand War Party.

No. 3. indicates the place to which all the people moved. The rites for the Small War Party were formed here.

Nos. 4 and 5 indicate another "move to new country" where the civil government was formed. The two Peacemaker clans were formed and a chief was taken from each of the two clans.

(This chart was drawn by Red Bird to illustrate the story of creating the Osage tribal government. Given in Smithsonian, BAE, 36th Annual Report.)

28

Legendary History of Organization

There is an allegorical story about the organization of Osage tribal government which has come down through the legends. (See Fig. 6.) This legend is supported by the myths and ceremonies. We are told that the first remembered government was military in form. For many generations several variations were tried with military government. Eventually it became clear that a civil government was also needed.

After the Wa sha she, the Hun ka, and the Tsi shu came to the earth they wandered over the land. In these wanderings the O su ka ha, They Who Make Clear the Way clan of the Wa sha she division led the way. After a very long time of wandering, the people were stopped by the Wa sha she because a village of unknown people was ahead. Hearing the large group of people, the strange people sent a messenger to find out what was desired. Only the Wa sha she entered the village for the Hun ka and Tsi shu found the filth and odor to be offensive.[2]

The leader of the strange people and the Wa sha she leader exchanged pipes. During their conversation the Wa sha she leader said, "I am Hun ka." At this remark the leader of the strange people held his right hand over his mouth, as a gesture of surprise, and then said, "I am also Hun ka." The strange Hun ka went on to explain that his people used the four winds for weapons and destroyed life wherever they found it. After the Wa sha she explained that his people wished to live with the strange Hun ka but they did not like to destroy life, he suggested that they all "move to a new country."[3] These three groups, Wa sha she, Hun

---

[2] Francis La Flesche, "The Osage Tribe: Rite of the Chiefs; Sayings of the Ancient Men," *Smithsonian Institution, 36th Annual Report,* (Government Printing Office: Washington, 1921), pp. 59-71.

[3] This expression meant, a reorganization of the existing government, although it may also entail a physical move. These strange Hun ka were called Hun ka u tah nun tse or Isolated Earth. Isolated Earth referred to an Osage belief that the earth was isolated from the other heavenly bodies. The Isolated Earth people came from the earth and not the sky.

29

ka, and Isolated Hun ka moved to fresh new land which was free of death. They united into a union of mutual defense. A House of Mysteries was placed in charge of the Isolated Hun ka. In this house the children were given their names. The house represented the earth. Another House of Mysteries was given to the Black Bear clan of the Hun ka. This house was dedicated to war.[4]

We have no clear evidence that the Tsi shu joined this union of the other three groups. We assume that if they did not unite at the same time, they joined a short time later. This is evident in the four pauses before attack and the four pauses before the hunt, that are a part of the war ceremonies. The War Party in Great Numbers or Grand War Party was instituted after the union and included all four groups.[5]

Evidently the first government of the Osage was dominated by the Isolated Hun ka. The Tsi shu possibly resented this and refused to join the alliance, but later relented and joined with the other three. Legends tell of a long time of almost continuous warfare and internal strife. Confusion among the people reached a critical point which prompted the Wa sha she to lead a "move to a new country."[6]

In this second step of the military government, the two Houses of Mysteries were left in the same hands. The Isolated Earth was still in charge of child-naming and the Black Bear was still in charge of the House of War. A slight addition was made in the latter; the Panther clan was added to the Black Bear clan as the keeper of the House of War. This clan, the Panther, was kindred to the Black Bear and acted as a vice-chairman of war matters.[7]

Authority to initiate war movements was vested in the four groups, that is, the Black Bear of the Hun ka, the Wa sha she, the

[4] La Flesche, *36th Ann. Rpt., op. cit.*

[5] *Loc. cit.*

[6] *Loc. cit.*

[7] *Loc. cit.*

Tsi shu, and the Isolated Earth. This also included the management of the grand hunts. It should be noted, that the Hun ka was represented by a single clan while the other three groups were represented directly. Another observation is worthy of consideration. The new arrangement severely curtailed the power of the Isolated Earth. Hunting involved killing and to the Osage, killing of any kind was classed as war.[8]

The first reorganization brought a much needed period of order and peace to the Osage. At first the reorganized military government was effective, however, as time passed it became so cumbersome with ceremonies that a rapid response to enemy intrusions could not be made. Again, a "move to new country" became necessary.[9]

By this time the Little Old Men had become an effective power within the tribal structure. Earlier, they had furnished the ideas for the tribal organization and had implemented the ceremonies. Yet, it was the Wa sha she division that had led the movements toward formation of the first two governmental organizations. The next reorganization was led by the Little Old Men.[10]

Final Military Government

To remedy the defect of delayed military response, the Little Old Men created the "small war party." The existing "grand war party" was left intact. This grand war party consisted of all four divisions, namely, the Wa sha she, Hun ka, Tsi shu, and Isolated Earth. It still required the elaborate ceremonies in the House of Mysteries. At this time a reorganization of the divisions was also made. The Wa sha she, Hun ka, and Isolated Earth became sub-

[8]*Loc. cit.*

[9]*Loc. cit.*

[10]*Loc. cit.*

divisions of the Hun ka grand division. This division represented the dry lands and waters of the earth. Another grand division was created from the Tsi shu and the Tsi ha she, Those Who Were Last to Come. This latter sub-division joined the original four divisions after the first reorganization. However, they were a part of the tribe at the time of this second reorganization. The Tsi shu grand division included the Tsi shu sub-division and Those Who Were Last to Come, and it represented the sky.[11]

Three classes of small war parties were created under this third military government. All three could be created "outside the House of Mysteries." This meant they could be formed without the time consuming ceremonies of the grand war party. The first class of small war parties was made up of warriors from only one of the grand divisions. A second type of small party consisted of warriors from at least two clans from either of the two grand divisions. Finally, a small war party could be formed by warriors from a single clan. It was under this last reorganization of the military branch of government that the Osages first met the white man. The military government had reached its final form with this reorganization, but the civil government was sorely in need of attention.[12]

Creation of the Civil Government

Weaknesses in the civil government did not become recognizable for several generations. Even when the problem was recognized, more generations lapsed before solutions were formulated and implemented. In order to keep the civil government separated from the military government, two new clans were created. These clans were denoted as peacemaker clans. Each of the two grand divisions had one peacemaker clan. A hereditary Tsi shu Chief was selected from the Tsi shu Peacemaker clan and a hereditary Hun ka Chief was selected from the Pon ka Peace-

[11]*Loc. cit.*

[12]*Loc. cit.*

maker clan.[13] The relationship between these two chiefs was similar to the relationship that exists between the English Cabinet and the Prime Minister. An English Prime Minister is a peer among equals. That is, while the two chiefs were equal in theory, the Tsi shu Chief was dominate in practice.

To forestall any seizure of total power by either or both chiefs, the Little Old Men carefully outlined the duties and powers of the chiefs. The twelve duties and powers can be placed in a list.

(1)   When any person engages in fighting and there is a threat to life, the chiefs must stop the fight.

(2)   If murder does occur and revenge upon the guilty one's life is sought, the chiefs must enforce the peace.

(3)   If a murderer, hunted by avengers, enters either of "the houses in the middle," or Chief's House, the chief is required to protect him.

(4)   The chief from the division of the murderer must require the guilty one to take gifts to the relatives of his victim as a peace gesture.

(5)   Refusal to make a peace gesture compels the chief to exile the murderer from association with the tribe. The chief is empowered to ask his people to give gifts to the relatives of the slain person, in this case.

(6)   Upon the continuing efforts of revenge seekers to take the life of a guilty person the chiefs must exile the determined avenger(s) from the village and tribe.

(7)   As sometimes happened, a person bent on revenge succeeded in killing the goal of his vendetta, after the chief had made peace between the two parties. When this happened, the chief was obligated to have the survivor(s) executed.

(8)   Any person whose life was threatened by another person could take sanctuary in "the house in the middle." The chief was duty bound to protect the threatened person's life.

(9)   The same rule applied to strangers, even though he may be an enemy. No bloodshed was allowed in either of "the houses in the middle."

[13]*Loc. cit.*

(10) Captives had to be brought to "the house in the middle" as soon as a war party returned. Here they were given their life and offered adoption. Some observers thought the Osages had slaves, which was a misconception. Captives were often given the honored office of Sho ka or messenger. They were preferred to Osage Sho ka s because they were considered to be more impartial. Possibly, some observers mistook these Sho ka s for slaves.

(11) Going to and from the grand buffalo hunts, the chiefs shared the responsibilities. It was the obligation of the chiefs to designate the route, the campsites, and departure times. While traveling, the chiefs served on alternate days. The Tsi shu chief would be in charge the first day, the Hun ka chief the second day, etc. until they reached the hunting grounds. There a ceremonially appointed director of the hunt took charge. This "chief" of the hunt served for a specific hunt; he was not a permanent official.

(12) To aid the chiefs in enforcement of their duties each were empowered to select five assistants called Ah ke ta s or Protectors, however, they were commonly called Soldiers by the white man. These soldiers had to be selected from any of ten clans but the chief was not required to select his five protectors from his own division. The soldier or protector clans were the Black Bear or Panther, Little Male Deer, Elk, Hun ka Having Wings, Isolated Earth, Men of Mystery, Buffalo Bull, Elder Tsi shu, Elder Sun Carriers, and Buffalo Bull Face.[14]

As we have stated above, the office of Ki he ka or chief was hereditary. The office was intended, by the Little Old Men to descend to the lineal male heir. If the male heir was disqualified for good cause, the nearest male kin in the line was selected. The Ah ke ta would form themselves into a council to determine who was the rightful heir to the chieftanship.[15] It should be noted, that,

[14] *Loc. cit.*

[15] *Loc. cit.*

the chief who was the head of the civil government was, with limitations, selected by a military group.

It seems evident that some additional duties and powers were given to the Tsi shu chief with the coming of the white men. Seemingly, the Tsi shu chief was given the duty of tribal spokesman to the white men. Evidently he acted as a special Sho ka, messenger, between the Little Old Men and the white men.

The Osage government, as presented here, existed in this final form until 1869. In that year, Isaac Gibson, the Osage Agent, suspended White Hair III as Tsi shu chief and appointed Paw ne no pa she, as Governor of the Osage.[16] The Little Old Men were decimentated by the white man's diseases and lack of qualified candidates. Their power was all but destroyed by the appointment of a council by Isaac Gibson early in 1871. The last of the Little Old men passed away in the early 1940's.

In its final form, before Isaac Gibson destroyed it, the Osage government placed the controlling power in the hands of the Little Old Men. All divisions and clans had representatives in this organization. Achievements, rather than votes, determined representation. Therefore, clans that produced outstanding warriors, scholars, statesmen, and priests were better represented than the clans that neglected to properly educate their young. It was a government of the elite, but admission to the elite was open to all men who excelled according to Osage ideals.

Separation of Civil and Military Powers

The Little Old Men were aware of the dangers inherent in military force. They employed several means to prevent a take over by a military cabal or junta. First, they provided a permanent civil government complete with an enforcement arm. Next, they

[16] Paw ne no pa she means, Not Afraid of the Pawnee. This man was also known as Big Hill Joe and Governor Joe. He was well educated at Osage Mission. In speaking of his education, Joe said, "It took the Jesuits thirteen years to make me a white man; it took the Osages three days to make me Indian again."

did not permit a standing army. True, virtually every Osage male trained for a lifetime as a soldier, and the Little Old Men themselves were the best soldiers of all. Yet, it must be noted that no permanent corps of officers existed. The power of appointing temporary officers resided in the Little Old Men. A final means of control was through the religious ceremonies; the Ancient Men were the only Osages who knew the rites. Without the ceremonies the military did not dare to take up the war path.

Executive Limitation

The executive power was divided between the two chiefs or retained by the Little Old Men. This was an effective means to keep one chief from seizing all the power to himself. The executive was also limited by "enumerated" powers. Resolution of succession problems was built-in by creating the council of Ah ke ta s. Each chief had only five Ah ke ta s as aides, which was hardly enough to engage in a coup d' etat, especially in a warrior society.

Judicial Powers

Some minor judicial power was given to the executives. However, these powers were limited to peace keeping matters, similar to those in the jurisdiction of a Justice of the Peace. Judicial powers were also given to the master of the hunt, but these were temporary and limited to violations of the rules of the hunt. In military activities similar judicial power was granted to the eight war party commanders. Yet, the major judicial powers were lodged in the Little Old Men.

The Military and the White Man

The seemingly uncontrolled raids of the Pomme Terre River Osages may or may not have been a sign of break-down in the control of the Little Old Men. We refer to the actions of the Osages who later became known as the Claremore bands. All through the late 1600's and 1700's, in fact up to their removal to Kansas in 1840, these Osages repeatedly raided traders and later the Cherokee immigrants.[17] These seemingly unchecked raids were a major cause of stalling the ambitions of the French and Spanish. Valid arguments could be made to support the idea that the Little Old Men instigated and condoned the raids. Equally valid arguments support the contention that these raids were conducted without the consent and support of the Little Old Men. Until conclusive evidence can be found, we cannot state with certainty that the Little Old Men had lost their control at this early date.

It seems unlikely that these raids during the 1700's were not controllable by the Little Old Men. To the contrary, it seems very likely they encouraged these raids as a part of their policy toward the French and Spanish. The Little Old Men were capable of playing the French and Spanish like a musician plays a fine instrument. They seemingly knew when and were to strike in order to inflict the greatest damage. Likewise, they apparently knew when to apply the light touch and beg for peace. The French and Spanish never suspected the Osage were capable of such diplomatic finesse. They were constantly kept off balance by rumors, probably started by the Little Old Men, that the Osages were preparing to form an alliance with the English. One must remember that these Little Old Men were proven warriors and masters of "bluff war." They possessed superior intellects and were experienced in dealing with other peoples. They also had at their command the largest military force in mid-America during the 1700's. In addition, they had the most effective coordinated government in mid-America during this same time span. This would include the mid-American governments of the English, French, and Spanish.

[17] An excellent account of the conflict between the Spanish and the Osages is given in, *The Imperial Osages,* Gilbert C. Din and Abraham P. Nasatir. See the bibliography.

Bibliography

Din, Gilbert C., and Abraham P. Nasatir, *The Imperial Osages: Spanish-Indian Diplomacy in the Mississippi Valley,* University of Oklahoma Press: Norman, 1983.

La Flesche, Francis, "The Osage Tribe: Rite of the Chiefs; Sayings of the Ancient Men," *Smithsonian Institution, Bureau of American Ethnology, Thirty-Sixth Annual Report,* Government Printing Office: Washington, 1921.

————, Francis, "The Osage Tribe: The Rite of Vigil," *Smithsonian Institution, Bureau of American Ethnology, Thirty-Ninth Annual Report,* Government Printing Office: Washington, 1925.

CHAPTER III

Religion

Introduction

There has always been a reluctance among the Osages to speak of the sacred rites. To preserve the myths and stories of the past, it was necessary for each new generation to learn them exactly as they were given to them. If they altered the forms in any way the original meaning would be lost. Therefore, the idea that these ceremonies must not be varied was impressed upon the minds of each new generation. This impression was so effective that it became customary to consider errors in reciting the rites outside the ceremonies as a sacrilege. Errors made within a ceremony could be corrected because of the checks provided in the ceremony. This fear of error and consequent punishment made the Osages reluctant to speak of the ceremonies.[1]

Although reverence for the rites was always present, mystic powers were not originally associated with the ceremonies. Any of the Little Old Men could act as priest, while all were intelligent and had retentive minds, some did not have inquiring minds. Those with inquiring minds were taught a body of legends in addition to the rites. From these legends they knew the ceremonies did not have mystic powers.[2] Yet, many of the Ancient Men and the people did believe the rites had mystic powers. Thus, the belief grew that if a person spoke irreverently of, or misused the rites or sacred objects a terrible penalty would fall upon them. Lest modern minds deem this belief a bit of ignorant superstition, let us

[1] Francis La Flesche, "The Osage Tribe: Rite of the Wa Xò Be," *Smithsonian Institution, BAE, 45th Annual Report,* (U.S. Government Printing Office: Washington, 1930), p. 29.

[2] *Loc. cit.*

examine some facts. No school of philosophy has ever been able to determine what is the ultimate reality. In the field of psychosomatic medicine, the mystery of how the mind affects the body has not been solved. The penalties the Osage refer to are psychosomatic. That is, the penalties are within the guilty person.

Given the "realities" of Osage culture, no intelligent modern mind should consider this Osage belief as mere ignorant superstition. Respect for others require respect for their customs. Therefore, one should not abuse that which is held in reverence by those who have different customs. The act of abusing what we do not appreciate, carries with it the punishment of ignorance.

In order to unfold the ancient Osage religion for the reader a paraphrase of the seven Wa ho pe rites will be given. These seven rites make up the Wa ho pe or War Ceremonies. The Peace Ceremonies will follow, but only parts of it will be given. The We ke a s, or prayers and the songs along with description of the presentation, would require many volumes of printed text. In order to compress the ceremonies, the We ke a s and songs are paraphrased.[3]

We must also note that the version paraphrased here is only one version. Although the basic forms, prayers, and songs agree, they vary somewhat depending on the division, sub-division, and clan. This variation, in detail, is done to fit the clan, sub-division, and division symbols and representations into the overall ceremony.

The Wa ho pe rites are divided into seven ceremonial divisions. None of the clans follow a single fixed order of the seven divisions, however, each clan had its own order. While the clans varied in the order of the first six divisions, the seventh was always the same division. We will use the Buffalo Bull version of

[3] Francis La Flesche, "The Osage Tribe: The Rite of Vigil," *Smithsonian Institution, BAE, 39th Annual Report,* (Government Printing Office: Washington, 1925), pp. 37-38.

the first rite as given by Tsa shin ka wa ti an ka, Saucy Calf.[4]

Overview

Buffalo Bull Order

(1) Singing the Wa ho pe Songs
(2) Making the Rush Mat for the Sacred Hawk
(3) Placing the Sacred Burden Strap Within[5]
(4) Songs of the Rite of Vigil
(5) Rite of Shooting a Bird
(6) Call to the Ceremonial Distribution of Scalps
(7) Songs of the Sayings of the Ancient Men

Songs of the Wa ho pe rite are presented in two major groups. The first group represent the Hun ka grand division and are called Wa lo Pa lo pa tsa or the Seven Songs. Wa lo Sha pa tsa or the Six Songs represents the Tsi shu grand division. There are eighteen songs in the first group and fifteen in the second group.[6]

The Seven Songs

(1) Songs of Opening the Shrine
(2) Songs of the Commander Standing at His Fireplace

[4] Francis La Flesche, "The Osage Tribe: Rite of the Chiefs; Sayings of the Ancient Men," *Smithsonian Institution, BAE, 36th Annual Report,* (Government Printing Office: Washington, 1921), p. 152; La Flesche, *45th Ann. Rpt., op. cit.,* p. 529.

[5] This "placing within" probably means placed in the list of tribal rites. A man honors his wife with this rite. She keeps the strap to the left or right of her door depending on her father's division.

[6] La Flesche, *45th Ann. Rpt., op. cit.,* pp. 541-542.

(3) Early Morning Songs
(4) Wolf Songs
(5) Isolated Hawk Songs
(6) Songs of Holding the Rattle
(7) Mysterious Song
(8) Songs of the Rite of Vigil
(9) Making of the Bow Songs
(10) Spirit Songs
(11) Midday Sun Songs
(12) Afternoon Songs
(13) Song of Ho ke (meaning obscure)
(14) Wanderings of the Wolf Over the Land Songs
(15) Weeping Songs
(16) Song of the Seizing (the counting of war honors)
(17) Crow Songs
(18) Buffalo Songs

The Six Songs

(1) Rising of the Buffalo Bull and Men Songs
(2) Deer Song
(3) Black Bear Songs
(4) Fight for the Symbolic Charcoal Songs
(5) Water Songs
(6) Star Songs
(7) Great Evening Songs
(8) Little Evening Songs, also called Owl
(9) Snake Songs
(10) Great Rain Songs
(11) Little Rain Songs
(12) Making them Strike Each Other Songs
(13) Songs of Drawing the Symbolic Arrows
(14) Victory Songs
(15) Songs of the Rising of the Participants

Skins

The Rite of Wa ho pe requires the skins of seven animals in its performance.

(1) Young mottled lynx [7]
(2) Dark gray wolf
(3) Male panther [8]
(4) Male black bear
(5) Large animal, buffalo
(6) Yellow animal, elk
(7) Little animal, deer

As a convenience to the reader we will use American terms for the officials of the ceremonies. The Ho ka was the initiator or official prompter, we shall call him Prompter. A Sho ka was a messenger, in this case a ceremonial messenger. We will call him Messenger. Another official was called Ah ke hon Ho ka or substitute prompter who acted as the Master of Ceremonies, however, we will refer to him as the Assistant. For the most part, the ceremonies were conducted by the Assistant and Messenger. In some parts, the Prompter was required to personally conduct the ceremonies.

The Seven Songs

Ceremony of Blowing on the Skins

This is the opening ceremony of the Wa ho pe degree. It is called Non ne ah la sho tsa, literally, tobacco smoking upon. The

[7] Shin ka normally means little, however, in ceremonies it often means young.

[8] Among the Osages, the cougar, puma, or mountain lion was called panther.

skins to be used in the ceremony were blessed by blowing tobacco smoke from the ceremonial pipe upon them.[9]

Shaping the Moccasins

At sunrise the day following the opening ceremony, Blowing on the Skins, the Little Old Men gathered for the second ceremony. This is called Hum pa su or Moccasins Cut. The cutting of moccasins refer to cutting out of the ceremonial moccasins worn by the Prompter and Messenger as a part of their priestly attire.

After all the Little Old Men are seated the Assistant gives the Messenger two pieces of buffalo hide. He also gives him a robe and other articles of value. The Assistant directs the messenger to lay these things in front of the headman of the Buffalo Bull clan. After the Messenger has carried out his instructions he kneels facing the headman with the buffalo hide between them.

Now the headman sets aside the gifts and starts reciting the Moccasin Ritual Prayer. All the members of the Buffalo Bull clan who are present also recite the prayer but not in unison. When the prayer is well started, the Messenger places a knife point near the center of one piece of buffalo hide. Without hesitation he acts like he is cutting a straight line to his right, which represents the east. He repeats this after a pause but pulls the knife toward himself, this "cut" represents the south. A "cut" is made for the west and finally, the north.

After a longer pause and while the recitation of the prayer continues, the squares are actually cut. They are cut along the same lines and same order as the pretended cuts. This first actual cut denotes a determination to kill the chief of the enemy tribe. The same procedure is continued for the remaining three cuts except a different person is figuratively killed. These are: A woman of an enemy tribe who is honored for her virtue and has nurtured a chief; an enemy warrior who is honored for his achievements in warfare; a woman of the enemy who has brought

[9] La Flesche, *45th Ann. Rpt., op. cit.,* p. 544.

44

her first child into life. These four "killings" are symbolism for the determination to destroy: (1) the enemy's leadership; (2) the enemy's organization; (3) the enemy's military power; and (4) the enemy's ability to prosper.

As the recitation of the prayer continues, the Messenger sews the left moccasin with six stitches. The use of the awl symbolizes the resolve to kill a young male enemy still in his teens. Tendons, used in the sewing, represent the deadly rattlesnake. The same procedure is followed with the right foot moccasin. This moccasin has seven stitches and stabbing with the awl represents the resolve to kill an enemy female in her teens. The tendon represents the red-bellied snake.

Now, as the recitation of the prayer continues, the Messenger fashions a second pair of moccasins as he did the first pair. This time an honored enemy is to be killed and the snake with a spotted belly is represented in the left moccasin. The other moccasin represents the slaughter of a woman who has birthed her first child and the snake with the white belly is symbolized.

Both pairs of these ceremonial moccasins are used by the Prompter in the rites. They symbolize the life journey of the Osage people. This journey through time is likened to the endless passage of the sun across the sky. The first pair represents sunrise and the second pair represents the sun's journey to the west.

Near the end of the prayer, the Messenger quickly makes a pair of moccasins for himself, which he will wear throughout the ceremony. These are made like the others. The awl symbolism is omitted, but the tendons represent the snake with a pink belly. Recitation of the prayer ends with the completion of this third pair of moccasins.

Reference to the Messenger's knife is made in the prayer. It symbolizes the left horn of a young bull. This was the Tsi shu side of the tribal organization. Likewise, the six stitches in the left foot moccasins were symbolic of the Tsi shu, while the seven stitches of the right foot moccasins were symbolic of the Hun ka. Thirteen stitches in each pair also suggest the possibility that the thirteen war honors were involved in these symbolic stitches.[10]

[10]*Ibid.*, pp. 547-550.

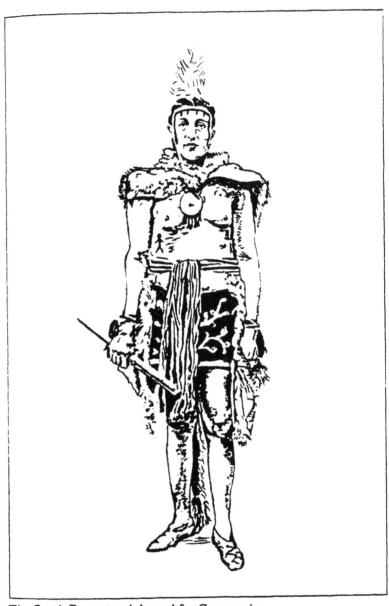

Fig. 7. A Prompter Adorned for Ceremonies
 *(Drawn from an illustration in Smithsonian, BAE, 45th Annual
 Report.)*

Adornment

This ceremony is called Ke non, the Adornment. It involves placing ceremonial symbols upon the Prompter.

Before the sun comes up on the next day after Shaping the Moccasins, the face of the Messenger is painted with charcoal. Then a deer tail head piece is placed on his head. The Messenger, carrying a filled "small pipe," informs the Prompter that the ceremony is about to begin. This message is delivered three times and the pipe is offered each time. If the Prompter accepts the pipe, it is taken as a vow that he will faithfully perform his ceremonial duties.

For a fourth time the message is delivered, but this time the Assistant accompanies the Messenger. The pipe is offered again and the Prompter smokes. When he finishes, the Assistant begins to recite the Adornment Prayer. He paints the face and body of the Prompter red as he recites the prayer. As the second part of the prayer is recited, a downy eagle feather is attached to the Prompter's scalplock, so the feather will stand erect. This feather has two meanings: (1) Wearing it is a symbolic prayer for a long life. (2) It stands for the beginning of day, dawn. (See Fig. 7.)

As the Assistant comes to the third part of the prayer, a white mussel shell disk attached to a buffalo hair neck string is hung from the Prompter's neck. A pair of woven buffalo hair wristbands are placed on the Prompter's wrists as the fourth portion of the prayer is recited. These wristbands symbolize the bonds of a captive. During the recitation of the fifth division of the prayer a panther skin robe is placed on the Prompter's shoulders. This is bound at the waist with a woven belt, called the captive's belt.

The final adornment is placed upon the Prompter's face. A black vertical line is drawn on both cheeks from the top of the forehead to below the mouth line. A horizontal line is drawn across the forehead from vertical line to vertical line. Four short vertical lines are then drawn from the horizontal line to the eyebrows. The short vertical lines are evenly spaced along the horizontal line. This completed symbol represented the earth and the four winds. The earth was pictured as a snare that caught all life and held it until death came. The winds bring rains and cold; warmth and life; one is tempted to say, they represented the trials and pleasures of life.

In another context, the vault of the sky is portrayed as a great head. The dome of the sky is compared to the crown of the head. It is interesting that the open end of the Prompter's snare has his mouth at the open end of the snare. In the great head allegory, spiritual life takes on a physical body as it leaves the allegorical head's mouth and comes to earth. After death, the spirit passes into the mouth and walks the spirit path or tongue, where it becomes reunited with the allegorical head or sky. With the addition of the snare and winds symbol, only a black drawing of a man on the right ribcage is necessary before the Prompter is ready for the next ceremony. This black figure represented the Prompter's spirit.[11]

The Footstep Prayer

A small ceremony transpires as the Prompter and officials approach the House of Mysteries. Primarily, the purpose is to teach the lesson that in all things the actions must be orderly. This is so the dignity of the people can be preserved and time can be given to thank the Great Creative Power for giving them life as a people. In essence, this is the meaning of the Footstep Prayer; the maintaining of order and respect for authority must be observed in all tribal affairs.[12]

Song of Opening the Shrine

When all is ready, the Prompter places his hands at each end of the shrine. This is the signal for the Assistant to start singing the

[11]*Ibid.*, pp. 554-555.

[12]*Ibid.*, pp. 558-563.

Wa ho pe Lu che or Untying the Shrine. While the song is being sung the Prompter turns the head of the shrine toward the Tsi shu then the Hun ka, this is done twice. Then the Prompter removes the carrying strap and without hesitation removes the woven buffalo hair outer covering. Likewise, he removes the deerskin middle cover and the woven rush inner cover. In removing these covers, the opening must be away from the Prompter and the withdrawal must be with a forward motion. All heavenly bodies move forward, never backward. The hawk shrine is removed from its bindings and brought forth as in a birth which the action symbolizes.

Standing at His Fireplace

The title of the next song is U tse U ke shin or Standing at His Fireplace. This song describes the leader of many people who are getting ready to break camp, to continue their travels at daybreak. The leader is standing by his fire as he issues his orders. Although this may apply to any leader, it especially applied to the main commander of warriors.[13]

Early Morning Song

The title of this song is Ko son en hre or Early Morning. This song is hymnlike in adoration of the principal adobe of Wa kon ta, the sun. Since the sun was a visible sign of Wa kon ta's presence, the Osage treasured its regularity and the incredible colors as it came into sight each morning. Its path across the visible sky struck them with wonder.

It was natural that the sunrise would be a frequent topic in the Osage ceremonies. The Early Morning Song depicts the symbolic birth of mankind. It likens the coming of the spirit of man from the

[13]*Ibid.,* p. 565.

49

darkness of spirit land into the light of day into physical bodies. Like human birth the head of the sun shows first followed by the arms or rays. The body then appears followed by the legs and feet or the remaining rays.[14]

Wolf Songs

These songs are titled Shon ka; the name means any of the three members of the dog family known to the Osage. While the dog and coyote were respected by the Osage, the Wolf was especially admired. In this title the wolf is the subject.

Eight men are the actual leaders of a grand war party, four from each grand division. In the songs, these men are called wolves. Traits of the wolf are attributed to these leaders. Wolves are always alert and tireless. In the pursuit of prey they are determined and energetic. Most of all, the wolf does not let "homesickness" deter him from his goal. This trait was the most difficult wolf trait for a warrior to emulate.

The songs represent a leader as speaking of the wolf and the passing day. They are an appeal to Wa kon ta to aid the leaders because they are limited in abilities. The leader desires the lasting quality of the daily sunlight. He also treasures the ability of the wolf to relentlessly range freely over foreign lands.[15]

Isolated Song of the Hawk

This ceremony is called Gra to Wa lo U kon tse or Hawk Song Standing Alone.

Because of his ability to soar on high and hover, the hawk was admired. This reminded the warrior to carefully explore before he attacked. The hawk's sharp vision was also a reminder to be alert. Courage, speed of attack, and the superb accuracy of the hawk's

[14]*Ibid.*, pp. 566-570.

[15]*Ibid.*, pp. 571-573.

strike, was stressed. Each of the eight commanders carried a Hawk Wa ho pe on his back so his followers could see it in an attack.[16]

Song of Taking the Rattle

The next song is called Pa ha Lu sa or Rattle Taking. Actually, this is a group of songs rather than a single song. It has one prayer and five songs. For the first time in the Wa ho pe ceremony the Assistant used the rattle. Up to this time the Assistant had beat the time by slapping his upper leg. At the same time the singers beat the time by clashing wooden wands together. The gourd rattle was used to beat time in all the remaining Wa ho pe ceremonies which followed.

Symbolism of the gourd rattle was the subject of the prayer in this group. The rattle represented a head which in turn symbolized (1) the head of the panther, which represented the relentless fire; (2) the head of a man, or allegorically, the Isolated Earth clan. The stones inside the gourd represented the teeth from the left or right jaw of the panther. Whether it was the left or right jaw depended on the grand division of the Assistant, Tsi shu would be the left jaw and the right would be Hun ka. Likewise, the handle represented the left or right forearm of the symbolic panther. Overall, the purpose of this ceremony and rattle was to stress that the people must be of one mind when they go to war.

The songs touch upon two themes. The first theme is a symbolic black hawk and a symbolic red hawk. In the song, the black hawk is mentioned first because it stood for the darkness where the great unknown resided. Next to be mentioned was the red hawk which represented the splendid color of day or the known world. The symbolic gray and little hawk are also mentioned as representations of the stars.

Another theme is the birth of man. Man was pictured as emerging from the darkness into the light of day. The last two

[16]*Ibid.*, p. 574.

51

songs touch on the marvel of this act. A note of distinction is made between man and animals. Man came from the unknown with the ability to think and speak, the animals did not. Thus, the ancestors of the Osage are called Men of Mystery.[17]

Rite of Vigil

These five songs are called No shin shon or Rite of Vigil. Pe she as used in the first song means mysterious, in normal use this means bad or evil.

The Little Old Men as representatives of the people, selects a To tun Hun ka or Sacred Leader of a war party. We will refer to him as the Leader. The Leader chooses a Prompter from his clan to instruct him in his duties as Leader. We must explain that the To tun Hun ka was a spiritual leader and not a physical leader of the war party. His function was to act as an intermediary between the people and warriors on one hand and Wa kon ta on the other hand. All Osage wars were, in a sense, holy wars so the Leader was the most important member of the war party. He received credit for victory and censure for defeat of the war party.

The Leader must go away from people and be alone. For seven days he must fast and use the minimum of sleep. He offers the prayers of the people to Wa kon ta. If at any time during the seven days he receives a sign that Wa kon ta has heard his prayers he may return to the village. If he returns after seven days and has received no sign, the war party is cancelled.

In another song, the Leader is represented as speaking. He speaks of the holy soil he puts on his forehead and hair. The earth is holy because it is an abiding place of Wa kon ta.

Another song speaks of facial adornment with soil applied by the Little Old Men. Their face and head are adorned with sacred signs. Blue soil is placed on the forehead and in the hair. A wavy line is placed on one cheek and a straight line on the other. The wavy line represents the portions of the earth north and south of

[17]*Ibid.,* pp. 576-585.

the sun's path. These are the areas touched by the life giving powers of the sun. The straight line represents the sun's path.[18]

Making the Bow

Me tsa Ka he or Making the Bow is the title of the next three songs. The first song tells of the ending of the ceremonies which created the war party, the bow has been made. Eight officers, four from each grand division, are selected to actually lead the war party. This leaves the Leader free to pursue his religious duties. The first two songs review the selection of officers and the symbolic weapons. All of these articles as well as captives and booty belong to the Leader.

In the last song, the Leader warns the enemy that the Osages in sober deliberations have decided to make war on them.[19]

Spirit Songs

These three songs are called Wa no he or Spirit. Among the Osages a firm belief in the presence of a soul was strong. The Ancient Men often brought out two inner entities in addition to the visible exterior physical entity. These three human entities were the soul, intellect, and body. Both men and animals possessed body and soul while only man could "explore with the mind" and verbalize his thoughts. Spirit as a word, conveys the meaning of soul and will or intellect. Yet, the Osage believed at times the spirit could speak through the "voice of the wind." This is the reason the Four Winds clan conducted the Spirit Songs. The songs were used in ceremonies other than the Wa ho pe or War Ceremonies. The dismissing of the spirit was always a part of any burial ceremony.

[18]*Ibid.*, pp. 586-592.

[19]*Ibid.*, pp. 593-595.

53

The Spirit Songs speak of the things mentioned above and more. They speak of the path which all living creatures must take into the unseen world at the end of their seen or physical life. Even the living, by living, are walking on the path to the unseen. Another song deals with the sorrow of the farewell, the sorrow of the departing spirit and the sorrow of those left behind.[20] Alfred, Lord Tennyson in Ulysses, captures very well the spirit of mankind making their farewells as they "strike out" into the unknown. The Spirit Songs capture this same concept.

> The lights begin to twinkle from the rocks;
> The long day wanes; the slow moon climbs; the deep
> Moans round with many voices. Come, my friends
> 'Tis not too late to seek a newer world.
> Push off, and sitting well in order smite
> The sounding furrows; for my purpose holds
> To sail beyond the sunset, and the baths
> of all the western stars, until I die.
> We are not now that strength which in old days
> Moved earth and heaven; that which we are, we are;
> One equal temper of heroic hearts,
> Made weak by time and fate, but strong in will
> To strive, to seek, to find, and not to yield.

Midday Sun Songs

Me Lo tun to, Sun Vertical or Vertical Sun is the title given to these songs. The Leader of the war party performs this rite. He performs this to seek a sign from the sun that the attack will meet success. It is performed near the enemy homeland where courage and divine support is most needed. Upon receiving an encouraging sign he takes the temporary title of Wa kon ta ke or Man of Mysteries. The songs conclude with the war party marching to battle confident of victory.[21]

[20]*Ibid.*, pp. 596-598.

[21]*Ibid.*, pp. 599-602.

Afternoon Songs

The next three songs have two names, Me Shin ka or Little Sun and Me Ah po ka or Downward Sun which we translate to afternoon. Whichever title one takes, the meaning is somewhat obscure. Possibly they are a reference to a point between night and day when the sun continues in all its glory beyond its zenith. A reference is made to the birth of the black hawk who was a much feared bird.[22]

Fish-Turtle Song

While the real meaning of the title of this song has been lost, the modern interpretation of the words is used. Ho ke, in modern Osage, means Fish-Turtle. This song is an introduction to the Wolf Songs which follow it. Its theme is traveling or wandering over the land; the word mo shon or land is used rather than hun ka.[23]

Wolf Songs

These two Wolf Songs are called Shon ka Mo shon Op she, literally, Wolves Lands March Upon or Wolves Who March Upon the Land. These songs tell of the authority of the eight temporal leaders to determine, in council, the route the war party will take each day. Only the four Tsi shu leaders are mentioned when one of their members act as Prompter. The four Hun ka leaders are the only ones mentioned when the Prompter is from that division. Each of the four wolves, the leaders, are portrayed as singing of his authority as a leader. The purpose is to impress upon the leaders their duties and responsibilities. It also stresses that they must be united in their decisions.[24]

[22]*Ibid.*, pp. 602-603.

[23]*Ibid.*, pp. 605-606.

[24]*Ibid.*, pp. 606-608.

Seizing the Wa to pa

Like many of the titles, this title is misleading to one unfamiliar with the ceremony. Its name is Wa lu sa or Seizing. In this ceremony the Wa to pa or warrior who has been chosen to count his war honors, is seized by his robe and "forced" to count his honors. This is done to protect the warrior's "modesty" about his achievements.

Before the Assistant begins to sing the songs he announces: "Ho! Little Old Men, I have come to the Seizing Songs. Now the Wa to pa is forced to come, O Little Old Men." As the warrior who has been selected is approached he pretends not to see or understand what is about to happen. When he is seized by the robe, he acts surprised that he was the one chosen. He is led to the Wa ho pe and given one bundle of six and another bundle of seven small twigs which still have the green leaves attached. As he counts each war honor, a twig is placed on the Wa ho pe.[25]

Dream Prayer

This prayer has been lost, Saucy Calf had not recited it for many years. Unwilling to give it in an imperfect form, he gave it in paraphrase. It means "things to dream on." This refers to the seven day vigil of the Leader of a war party. The prayer mentions signs by which the Leader will know that Wa kon ta has heard his prayers.[26]

Wailing Songs

The Assistant would sing the Wa en ha ka, Wailing Song, and the women would begin to wail as the Little Old Men recited the dream prayer. Women who had taken their husband's place

[25]*Ibid.*, pp. 608-610.

[26]*Ibid.*, pp. 610-614.

among the Little Old Men wailed for their lost husbands.

When the Dream Prayer and Wailing Song were finished and all was quiet, the Wa to pa was asked to retrace his steps. At this time the Wa to pa or warrior selected, counted his war honors as mentioned in the Seizing of the Wa to pa ceremony. The Little Old Men of the three sub-divisions, earth, water, and sky, recited the three versions of the counting twigs for war honors. These were the thirteen footprints of the black bear, the thirteen sun's rays, and the male beaver and thirteen willow twigs.[27]

Song of the Wa to pa

The second song has two stanzas. The words are addressed to the Wa to pa, the man chosen by the candidate to recount the deeds he performed when he fought in defense of the tribe.

By the first stanza, the honored warrior is commanded to go to the place prepared for him, there to travel again the path of honor he had made in his warlike career.

In the second stanza the honored warrior is commanded to go to the seat of honor and there count, one after the other, the thirteen war honors he has won, in accordance with the tribal rites.[28]

Crow Songs

These two songs are called Ka ha or Crow Songs. These songs picture a battlefield with the slain of both sides strewn about. The crows come two by two for a feast upon the bodies. Their fights for bits of the bodies precede their departure as they came, two by two. A crow belt is worn by some Siouan tribes by especially brave warriors. The crow belt commemorates the Crow Songs.[29]

[27]*Ibid.*, pp. 614-616.

[28]*Ibid.*, pp. 619-620.

[29]*Ibid.*, pp. 621-623.

Buffalo Songs

In Osage, the buffalo is called Tsa. There are twelve songs in this group of songs. Two concepts run throughout the songs, the coming of the buffalo and the gift of corn. These two foods were the mainstay of the Osage diet. From the songs, it is evident that the buffalo preceded corn as the major source of Osage food.

As the Buffalo Songs are about to start the Assistant announces: "Little Old Men! I have come to the Buffalo Songs. On arriving at these songs it is customary to have the Ke non present, O Little Old Men!" The Ke non is symbolic painting or adornment. At this time the Messenger brings the wife of the candidate and her friends into the House of Mysteries. She must be present to receive instructions in the planting of ceremonial corn.

The songs start with the coming of the buffalo from the mysterious world of darkness into the physical world of light. This is symbolic of all creation. Both male and female were created with full powers of reproduction. The birth of the buffalo calf is also depicted. With the appearance of the male, female, and calf, the act of creation is complete. A mood of reflective thought is projected by the song as well as a feeling that this creation is an event of great importance to the people. This is followed by a song of joy for the gift of the buffalo.

A part of these Buffalo Songs is called the Corn Songs. The Corn Songs do not touch upon the myth of how the Osage got the corn originally. They sing the praise of women who plant and care for the corn as she does for her children. The coming of the warm spring sun brings the earth to life, smoke rising from burning vegetative debris as the fields are cleared help picture the preparation for planting. At last the rows of hills are planted and the hopes of an abundant harvest are evident in the songs. Now the seeds sprout and send blades from the darkness into light. With roots in darkness and stalks in the light, the corn combines sky and earth to create new life. In this reawakening of life was the presence of the Creative Power which was symbolized by the

58

woman's footprint on the corn hill.[30]

The Six Songs

Stand-by of Men, Buffalo Songs

These four songs are called Tsa to ah Ne ka e No shin, Buffalo Men Stand-by or Stand-by of Men, Buffalo Songs. These songs are, in many ways, a continuation of the previous Buffalo Songs. However, a new theme is the "rising" or getting to their feet, of the buffalo as they prepare to enter the daylight of the known world. This same theme applies to men. The tones of the music are ones of elation.[31]

Deer Song

In modern Osage, Tah is the word for deer, in some of the ceremonies, an archaic form is used for deer, this is Tah hre. Since the Osages considered gall as the source of courage, it seems strange they would choose the deer as a symbol of courage. The deer has no gall bladder and the Osages were aware of this. Although the deer was not a courageous animal, it was admired for its swiftness. For this reason, it was given an important place in the war rites. These are the things mentioned in the song.[32]

Black Bear Songs

These Wa sop pe or Black Bear Songs are the last to be held in the House of Mysteries before the war party leaves. This is the

[30] *Ibid.*, pp. 623-639.

[31] *Ibid.*, p. 643.

[32] *Ibid.*, pp. 644-645.

opening and closing theme of these songs. A theme in between is the charcoal which must be ceremonially prepared. The warriors must wear this symbol of ruthless fire when they attack for if it is not on their face, any honors they earn will be ignored. When these songs end, it is a signal to the warriors that they must prepare to move against the enemy. Both the Black Bear and Panther are symbols of the ruthless fire, hence these are called Black Bear Songs. The Black Bear represents both clans.[33]

The Rush for Charcoal

These three songs are called No gra e ke tsa or The Rush for Charcoal. This ceremony is a shortened version of The Rush for Charcoal used in the Grand Wa ho pe. The Hawk Wa ho pe or ceremony of the portable shrine is the ceremony we have been outlining. It is used in the three classes of small war parties. Two huge fires of red bud or red willow are built before dawn. Gathered around the fires are the warriors.

The war standards, four dark and four light, are given to the eight leaders. As the rattles beat faster and the singers sing louder the warriors dance. Both the Prompter and the Assistant call out: "Dance young man! You may never have another chance to dance before these people!" Then the signal to rush the fire is given. Upon this signal the warriors rush the fires seizing burning sticks to secure a supply of charcoal. At times the warriors struggle with each other for choice pieces.[34]

Water Songs

The Ne tse or Water Songs are sung as a prayer by a war party when they come to a dangerous river crossing. The eel is appealed

[33]*Ibid.*, pp. 646-653.

[34]*Ibid.*, pp. 654-657.

to as well as the beaver, otter, and large turtle. All of these were known to be powerful swimmers. To protect their bowstrings, food supply, and shrines small boats made of the skins of these animals were made when crossing a dangerous stream. Three land animals were appealed to because they too were strong swimmers. These were the black bear, the panther, and the gray wolf.[35]

Star Songs

Wa tsa is the ancient word for stars, it is commonly used in the ceremonies rather than Me ka ke, the modern Osage word for star. In the two songs which belong to the Buffalo Bull clan, the songs refer to the Morning Star. The Elder Tsi shu songs mentions the Red Star or Polaris and "The Wolf or Dog that Hangs at the Side of the Heavens" or Canis Major.[36]

The Great Evening Songs

These songs are Pa se to Tun ka or Great Evening Songs. What role these songs play in the ceremonies is a mystery. Possibly one of the splinter tribes carried the meaning with them when they splintered. The answers may be in the ceremonies of the Omaha, Ponca, Kaw, or Quapaw. Since they are brief, they are given below in a free translation.

Song One

1.

To the people of the night I am going
To the people whose foreheads bear a mystic mark.

2.

To the people of the night I am going
To the people on whose bodies there are mystic marks.

[35]*Ibid.*, p. 658.

[36]*Ibid.*, p. 659.

61

Song Two

1.

There are peoples of the night, you have said,
Peoples whose foreheads bear a mystic mark.

2.

There are peoples of the night, you have said,
People on whose bodies there are mystic marks.[37]

Little Evening Songs

This group of songs is called Pa se to Shin Ka or Little Evening Songs. These songs have another name which is Wa po ka or Gray Owl Songs. The gray owl is often seen in the early evening. In these three songs the Leader is represented as speaking. This Leader camps alone, away from the war party. In the evening he listens for the sounds of the gray owl, horned owl, and wolf for signs that his prayers have been heard.[38]

Snake Songs

These songs are called We tsa, literally, He Who Kills, but freely translated as Snake Songs. These songs refer to the venomous snakes. Abilities to lie concealed and strike with deadly speed were coveted by the warriors. Rattlesnakes and all other poisonous snakes are included in the songs for this reason. At times the snake speaks in the songs.[39]

[37]*Ibid.*, p. 661.

[38]*Ibid.*, pp. 663-664.

[39]*Ibid.*, pp. 665-668.

The Great Rain Songs

The Ne shu Tun ka or Great Rain Songs include a prayer and three songs. Penalities are the themes of the prayer. These penalities hung over the head of one who gave a sacred promise to not misuse the rites. If his oath was violated, the penalities rained down on him.

The avengers are the swallow, the great dragonfly, and the great butterfly. These avengers have the power to detect that which is hidden, therefore, a person who violates his vow cannot conceal from them his evil act. Since all three are associated with an approaching thunderstorm, great rains, they are included in these songs.

Thunderstorms in the Osage homeland are truly awe inspiring. The crashing thunder and blinding lightning alone, are enough to excite the heart. Winds, hail, and incredible downpours of rain add to the reminder that man is a very small weak creature. We find both humility and respect for nature in this group of rain songs.[40]

The Little Rain Songs

The Ne shu Shin ka or Little Rain Songs are one of the most dramatic in the Wa ho pe ceremonies. Enactment of striking the earth brings the lessons of sky and earth to the forefront in a forceful fashion.

First, the earth is struck with a war club, this act and the dent made, represent the seizure of the sky by the earth. Next, a straight line is drawn, with the club, to the west. This straight line represents the sun's path from midday to sunset and another straight line to the east represents the sun's path from sunrise to midday. Two wavy lines are drawn, one to the north and one to the south. The sun's life giving touches are represented by these wavy lines. Thus, the sky and earth were symbolically brought together.

[40] *Ibid.*, pp. 669-671.

As soon as striking the earth ends, a branch of a cottonwood tree is set in the central dent of the design made. The cottonwood tree represents the continuity of life. As the song begins the Prompter touches, lovingly, the cottonwood tree first on the west, then the north, the east, and finally the south. This same sequence is followed as he snaps a leaf end from each side. By this act the Prompter symbolizes the distribution of life over the earth. In the last action all the limbs are broken from the tree and the pieces are then thrown backward over the Prompter's shoulder as he faces the east. This act represents the natural end of life.[41]

Releasing the Arrows Songs

These songs are called Moh gru Stet se or Releasing the Arrows Songs. The theme of these songs is the continuance of the tribe and the individual member in a perpetual line. Two arrows, one red and one black, are released to continually chase the setting sun. The bow is also red and black. Red, in this case, represents the day and black the night.[42]

Songs of Making One Strike the Other

In Osage, these songs are called Ke ka he e ke tse, which in a free American translation means Making One Strike the Other. The Leader mentions the red hawk and black hawk as aiding him when the war party is facing a dangerous foe. The next song pictures the warriors returning home victorious and bringing the Hawk Wa ho pe s home with them.

During the last song the Prompter places a scalp on the ceremonial club and holds them in his left hand. Then in his right hand he takes up a Wa ho pe. He then dances and sings of the

[41]*Ibid.*, p. 675.

[42]*Ibid.*, pp. 672-674.

64

victorious black and red hawks. Suddenly, he gently strikes the scalp with the Hawk Wa ho pe. This act indicates that an Osage warrior will always defeat the tribal foes.[43]

Victory Song

Wa tse ah tse or Victory is the name of this song. To a great extent this is a continuation of the hawk themes in the preceding songs. The song tells us the hawk is the child of the sun and the moon.[44]

Song of Closing the Ceremony

This last song is called U lu se e no shin, a free translation would be, Song by Which the Participants of the Ceremony Rise to Go Home. The Little Old Men rise and march out in ceremonial order. This ends the Wa ho pe ceremony.[45]

Parts of the Wa ho pe Rites are used in other ceremonies and on occasions other than war. At times, where peace is involved, the references to bloodshed and war are omitted. To illustrate some of the occasions where parts of the Wa ho pe Rites are used and modified, we will present an example.

Uses of the Rite of Vigil

The Rite of Vigil or No shin Shon, Stand to Sleep, is used in at least five different situations. These are listed below.

(1) This rite was used by the entire tribe three times each day, at dawn, at midday, and at sunset. Dawn was represented by

[43]*Ibid.*, p. 676.

[44]*Ibid.*, p. 677.

[45]La Flesche, *39th Ann. Rpt., op. cit.*, p. 41.

the red eagle, midday by the white eagle, and sundown by the bald eagle.

(2)   We have mentioned its use in the early parts of the Wa ho pe ceremony.

(3)   It may be used by an individual as part of the mourning period. An individual in exile for the murder of a neighbor may take the rite as a gesture of atonement for violating tribal law.

(4)   When a man is initiated into the mysteries of Weaving of the Portable Shrine he takes the Rite of Vigil.[46]

(5)   Women who weave the Wa ho pe cover also take the rite.

Penalities

The guardians of the penalities are interesting both in variety and nature. A hint that the penalities were mainly within an individual was given in an earlier chapter. These penalities will be given in a free translation after the guardians.

Spirits of four animals were guardians of the penalities. These were: (1) the mottled lynx, (2) male panther, (3) black bear, and (4) elk. Four birds were guardians: (1) swallow, (2) mottled eagle, (3) nighthawk, and (4) bank swallow. Two insects were frequently mentioned as guardians, these were the great dragonfly and great butterfly. Only one inanimate object was named as a guardian, this was the ceremonial "Little Pipe." It is interesting to note the absence of vegetative and elemental guardians. Only spiritual, animate life and a ceremonial object are mentioned.

Some of the penalities are given in the Penalities Prayer.

My grandfather (Great Butterfly)
Overtakes them and makes them to become languid,
    to seek solitude and sit in wretchedness,
Verily, he makes them to become restless and to lie here
    and there in distress.

[46]*Ibid.*, pp. 41-50.

My grandfather,
Causes them to fail to reach the four divisions of
    the days. (four stages of life)
My grandfather,
Even causes them to lose consciousness and never
    to recover.
He even takes from the guilty their spirit (sanity)
    when bidden to do so.[47]

These penalities above were used by all divisions and clans.
Others were used by specific clans.

Sending of Will Power

When a Leader, the eight commanders, and warriors of a war party were ready to go off to war, they would say goodbye to their kith and kin. They would simply say, "I go" or "I am going." To the Osages, these words had a larger meaning than they do in the American culture. They not only carried the departure meaning but at the same time conveyed a request. The request was, "I may never return so send me your will power while I am gone." In times of danger, the Osages believed by exerting their will, courage and strength of one person could be sent to another.

Sham War

Introduction

An excellent example of adapting a ceremony from one purpose to another is present in the Sham War. This is a part of the Peace Ceremonies and also illustrates the fun loving side of

[47]*Ibid.*, p. 111.

Osage religious practices. Like the Greek theater, and life itself, the Osage religion encompassed both tragedy and comedy.

The sham war begins with the coming of two "strangers" these were actually two men who pretended to be strangers who ride into the village. They are seated and given food and gifts. The food is devoured rapidly as though the "strangers" were famished. While the "strangers" are gulping the food, members of the ceremony are making remarks about them. These remarks are usually observations and comments meant to be comical. For example: "They are hungry, they have traveled far." "Yes, see how worn their moccasins are." "The tall one looks like an Isolated Earth." "The short one wears his hair like an Elder Tsi shu."

Without any change of expression, or notice of the remarks, the "strangers" complete their meal. With exaggerated gestures they indicate they are finished and are ready to "talk." They are then asked, in finger talk, where they are from. The "strangers" then pretend to converse together in a strange tongue, and then both gesture to the west and draw in the hands with the index finger upward. This indicates they come from the unknown and the erect index finger means they walk the spirit path back to the unknown. Remarks such as, "The tall one smells like a skunk" which is a symbol of the Isolated Earth follows these gestures.

After this joking episode is finished, the "strangers" inform the people, in finger talk, that a large enemy war party is approaching the village. After informing the people of the impending attack the "strangers" thank them for the food and gifts. Then they leave and continue their journey.

Immediately, a crier walks through the village. He cries out, "Ho! Two war parties have been reported. They plan to attack us. Young warriors, defend your people, prepare to fight them."

Name Taking

Young men and boys love to take part in farces. They rush to their maternal uncles as soon as they hear about the coming attack. Before they go, a gift of value must be provided for the uncle. Clutching the gift they run to their uncle and give him the gift. Then the boy would say: "Uncle I beg you, give me a name to use in the attack." Since the maternal uncle never jokes with his nephew, they both make the most of this one exception to the custom. The uncle may respond with: "Ho! Your name will be, He Who is Last to Arise." If the boy has been eyeing the girls, the uncle may say: "Ho! My nephew, I have a name for you, you shall be, He Who Chases Girls." Even in fun, these uncles felt the responsibility for teaching their nephews. For example, perhaps a boy had not been properly caring for his pony, the uncle may say: "Ho! My nephew your gift is beautiful. I will give you a beautiful name. Your name is, Sore Back."

The young men and boys proclaim their names throughout the village. All through the evening and into night the nephews are the good-natured subjects of jokes about their new names. Thus, their faults and failings are stressed not in censure, but in fun. As the night deepens, one by one, the "warriors" go to bed.

The coming of the "strangers" and name taking are part of the Wa wa lo or Peace Ceremony. These had a purpose in the schemes of the Ancient Men. It was hoped that the fun and good spirit of the ceremonies would foster a good feeling toward each other as well as strangers. Preparations for the "attack" resumed before daylight the next morning.

Charcoal Fight

Some significant changes are made in the peace version of the Charcoal Rite of the Wa ho pe Ceremony. Only the symbolic swan, golden eagle, and deer are mentioned in the peace version. The black bear and panther are omitted because they always stand for war and never peace. Another omission is the expression, "it has been said in this house." This expression is at the end of each line in the Wa ho pe Ceremony. Since it refers to the

House of Mysteries dedicated to war, it is omitted from the Wa wa lo Ceremonies. The expression, "it has been said" is used instead of including, "in this house." When the expression, "it has been said" is used, it refers to the House of Mysteries which is dedicated to peace.

The symbolism of the charcoal is also changed in the Peace Ceremonies. Instead of representing the unrelenting, ruthless fire that destroys all in its path, the meaning of the charcoal is changed to a peaceful symbol. The free translation is, "Black indeed, shall be the charcoal they make for themselves, throughout their life's journey." In meaning, this is saying only through unity could people bring peace and good will to all men. Therefore, the charcoal becomes a symbol of the effort toward peace. As a war symbol charcoal also carries this symbolism since, at least in Osage theory, the purpose of war was to establish and stabilize the peace.

As in the Wa ho pe Ceremony, when the signal is given to rush for the charcoal the young men and boys come from all directions. Brands and coals are kicked with reckless abandon amidst shouts and war whoops. Once they have secured the charcoal the boys and young men paint their faces. They also paint their hourses, which they now mount to repel the "attack."

The Attack

They go to the end of a level place about a mile in length. Placing themselves in a line and all facing the length of the meadow, they "charge" when the signal is given. Whips fly and heels thump into the ponies as they are urged to run. The party makes for the Hun ka House of Mysteries which is a house of peace. Each "warrior" carries a wand as a "weapon." This is a weapon that brings gifts, peace, and happiness. If one of the "defenders" manages to touch the House of Mysteries with his wand, he wins the gifts inside.

Conclusion

After the "attack" is repulsed all gather for the closing ceremony. The blankets and other gifts, that was in the House of Mysteries, are distributed among the young men and boys who were the valiant "defenders." Upon receiving his gift, each boy must shout out the name given to him by his maternal uncle.[48]

[48]Francis La Flesche, "War Ceremony and Peace Ceremony of the Osage Indians," *Smithsonian Institution, BAE, Bulletin 101,* (U.S. Government Printing Office: Washington, 1939), pp. 233-242.

Bibliography

La Flesche, Francis, "The Osage Tribe: rite of the Chiefs; Sayings of the Ancient Men," *Smithsonian Institution, Bureau of American Ethnology, Thirty-Sixth Annual Report,* Government Printing Office: Washington, 1921.

_____, Francis, "The Osage Tribe: The Rite of Vigil," *Smithsonian Institution, Bureau of American Ethnology, Thirty-Ninth Annual Report,* Government Printing Office: Washington, 1925.

_____, Francis, "The Osage Tribe: Rite of the Wa Xo' Be," *Smithsonian Institution, Bureau of American Ethnology, Forty-Fifth Annual Report,* U.S. Government Printing Office: Washington, 1930.

_____, Francis, "War Ceremony and Peace Ceremony of the Osage Indians," *Smithsonian Institution, Bureau of American Ethnology, Bulletin 101,* U.S. Government Printing Office: Washington, 1939.

CHAPTER IV

Marriage, Child Naming-Adoption, and Education

Marriage

Introduction

After Indian Territory became the State of Oklahoma in 1907, the Osages accepted the monogamy rules of the American culture. While the ceremonies still included more than one wife, all but one was a symbolic wife after Statehood. This practice of symbolic wives was still in use as late as 1932.[1] Some older Osage men had more than one wife in 1907 and continued to live with multiple wives until they died.

We must keep in mind that cultural customs and mores are the products of the environment in which they evolved. Osage women have, historically, always outnumbered Osage men. At least two statistics show this to be true. (1) The Osage Annuity Rolls from 1847 to 1890 show the female birthrate to be nearly twice that of the male birthrate. (2) The survival rate in the fifty to sixty-year-old bracket show between three and four females for every male in the age group. A greater spread is shown among those over sixty years of age.

No one pretends that Osage women had an easy life. Yet, it is interesting, that in the American culture, during the 1840's men outlived their wives as the census schedules show. Almost without exception those who recorded Osage life mentioned the

---

[1]Mrs. Rose Tinker Watkins related that she had stood as a symbolic second wife in such a marriage.

hard lot of Osage women. However, if they mention the life of the men, it was to portray their easy life. To a casual observer this would seem to be true, especially if the observer was using the European cultural standards as the measure.

John Hunter, a white captive among the Osages in the late 1700's, gives us some clues. He repeatedly mentions that Osage warriors pushed themselves so hard physically that they often coughed up blood. Long ceremonial fasts, hunts without food, and long periods without sleep served to weaken Osage men. Hunter also mentioned that when food was scarce the men only ate once a day so the women and children would have food.[2] If one adds to this those killed in warfare and the hunt, it is easy to see why there were fewer men than women. These were all factors affecting Osage polygamy.

Because of marriages involving more than one wife and a male dominance, lineages were always traced through the male line. To avoid close intermarriages the man and woman must be from different divisions than their own and of their parents.[3] In order to further restrict the possibility of intermarriage, it was customary to marry all the sisters in a family. Two exceptions to this rule was common. (1) A man in later life, sometimes married his brother-in-law's, wife's brother's, daughter. (2) If he had no wife or only one wife, he was expected to marry his brother's widow.

A young Osage male would have been disgraced if he showed a special feeling for any single female. He had to earn war honors before permitting himself to show a preference for a particular woman. Certainly, lifelong attachments were sometimes formed in childhood, but this must be hidden until the proper time arrived to expose these feelings. Even courting must be limited to respect

---

[2] John D. Hunter, *Manners and Customs of Several Indian Tribes*, (Ross and Hains, Inc.: Minneapolis, MN 1957), pp. 206-207.

[3] Francis La Flesche, "The Osage Tribe: Rite of the Chiefs; Sayings of the Ancient Men," *Smithsonian Institution, BAE, 36th Annual Report*, (Government Printing Office: Washington, 1921), p. 51.

and inquiries about the lady's state of health.[4]

The Osages had two forms of recognized marriages. These were called Me shin or The Unmarried and O me ho or Married Before. A third type of mating was called Ka shon le me gro ka or To Enter Matrimony Recklessly. This last type was not a recognized marriage. Marriages of the first two types are probably still legal under American law. We are not aware of any changes in law that would declare them illegal.

Me shin

This ceremony was for the young man and young woman or Tsa ka no, New Grown as they were called. Actually any marriage of a man and woman who had never married before was called Me shin regardless of age. Since most Osages married young, the chance of a first marriage for mature men and women was rare. Puberty was considered to be a marriageable age. From this time until they were married the two sexes were kept apart.

Much has been written about the parents and especially the maternal uncle selecting a bride for a young man. This leaves the impression that the young person's wishes were not asked for or considered. In some cases, this was probably true. However, in a majority of the marriages the preference of the young man and woman were the most important consideration. Yet, there were other important factors which both sets of parents and uncles considered. Marriage within the clans of the father and mother was forbidden. Were the parents of the man and woman properly married? Genetics was a consideration of importance.

While size was by no means a consideration in all families, in others it was a marriage factor. A family who prized tallness would rarely allow a tall offspring to marry a short mate. While the Osages recognized diet as a factor in tallness, they were also aware that tall parents often produced tall offspring. The prowess of a mother and father in providing food was deemed a good

[4] Hunter, *op. cit.,* pp. 243-244.

recommendation since they were good providers. Tallness in parents and offspring was also adjudged a worthy attribute. It was not without reason that the Osages were dubbed "giants of the prairies."

Parents of the young man made the first overtures toward marriage. Custom forbade a leading suggestion from a young lady's family. When a suitable young lady had been found who was agreeable to the young man's family, four Ne ka To ho or Good Men were called. In common usage, Log ny means good and Ne ka is the word for man. To ho is the archaic ceremonial word for good. In order to merit the honor of this title at least three generations must have lived according to tribal custom. That is, the man's parents, he and his wife, and their children.

These four Good Men were paid for their services in arranging the details of the marriage. Contrary to the popular view, Osage brides were not "purchased." Gifts between the two families were exchanged. It was the duty of the Ne ka To ho to carefully evaluate the gifts to be sure none of the relatives on either side would be offended. After the gift exchange problems were settled the prospective bride's family asked the Good Men to notify the prospective groom's family that the relatives would consider the marriage. Before the next action was set in motion either side could in good grace refuse the marriage.

Approval of the maternal uncles of the young man and young woman was sought at this time. Customarily, only one of the maternal uncles of the boy and of the girl was consulted. This was the uncle that had been their mentor and advisor as they were growing up. Usually this was the oldest maternal uncle of each the boy and girl. If the uncle agreed to the marriage, the girl's parents sent a messenger to the boy's parents notifying them of their consent and a time for gift giving.

At the time given, the groom's parents led their relatives to the bride's lodge. When all the gifts had been given to her relatives, the boy's relatives went home. The following day the bride was escorted to the home of the groom. She was often escorted by her uncle, but more often by the headman of her clan. This "delivery of the bride" was, in effect, a way of saying, "We give to you our daughter." The bride then distributed her gifts to the groom's relatives.

On the next day the bride and groom led a parade of the groom's relatives to the home of the bride's parents. This completed the marriage because the groom's parents by delivering their son to the bride's parents were saying, "We give to you our son."[5]

A great deal of variation existed from this point. At times the newlyweds set up their own households and this seemed to be the predominant practice. However, the evidence certainly indicates some newlyweds resided with either the bride's parents or with the groom's parents. A few faint clues indicate the ancient custom required the newlyweds to live a year in the lodge of the bride's parents. Equally faint clues indicate the ancient custom was to live in the lodge of the groom's parents.[6] These may have been sub-division or clan customs. However, the Annuity Rolls of 1878 clearly show all three arrangements were used at that date.

O me ho

The name O me ho means in a free translation, Those Who Have Married Before. At least one of the parties to this marriage must have been married before in a Me shin marriage. This O me ho marriage was for widows, widowers, and divorced persons. Marriages between spinsters and never married bachelors would be by a Me shin marriage.

Arrangements and required forms of conduct were much less complicated in an O me ho marriage than in a Me shin marriage. A man who wished to marry a widow or divorcee sent a

[5] Francis La Flesche, "Osage Marriage Customs," *American Anthropologist,* ns. 14:127-130, 1912.

[6] Louis F. Burns, *The Osage Annuity Rolls of 1878, First Roll, Second Roll, and Third Roll,* (Ciga Press: Fallbrook, CA, 1980).

messenger to her with his proposal and a gift. If her parents and uncle were dead, she sent the messenger to her nearest living relatives. If the relatives or, as the case may be, her parents approve, the messenger was sent to the man to notify him of their approval. Then the messenger escorted the man to the woman's lodge and the groom seated himself beside the bride. By sitting side by side in this manner they were married. The groom paid the messenger a fee for his services and only the bride received a gift.[7]

Ka shon le Me gro ka

Ka shon le Me gro ka may be freely translated as, Those Who Have Married Recklessly. Literature and history give us many examples of lovers defying taboos and physical barriers. While the Osages did not condone "common law" marriages, they recognized that young lovers would sometimes become "reckless." If parents discovered their children living in this "state of nature," the boy and gifts were immediately sent to the girl's parents. Thus, they were considered to be married as though by Me shin.

However, if a child was in evidence or for some reason they did not marry by tribal custom, a terrible penalty fell on the couple. First, the male involved could never acquire the title of Good Man or Honorable Man. Thus, he could never become a Little Old Man. Finally, the children coming from this "natural state," could never receive a clan name and, therefore, could never be a person. That is, although they were of Osage blood they were not of the Osage tribe. Living in a "natural state" was considered to be the act of animals. Humans who lived this way were considered to be animals, not persons, and their children were treated as the young of beasts.[8]

[7] La Flesche, *Am. Anth., op. cit.*

[8] *Loc. cit.*

Cultural Conflicts in Marriage

Akin to this line of reasoning is another matter. Early and even later marriages between other races and the Osage raised serious questions. As sometimes happened an Osage girl cohabitated with a white trapper or trader. Among the Osages this was regarded as Ka shon le Me gro ka. Exactly the same as would have been the case if both had been Osage. However, as more often it happened, an Osage girl would marry a white man in a Me shin marriage.

Since a child could only receive a name in his father's clan and the white father had no clan, unless he was adopted, the child could not be named. Again we find a non-person of the blood but not of the tribe. If the situation was reversed and the father was Osage but the mother was white, there would be no problem in child naming. This, of course, is assuming the marriage was Me shin or O me ho.

Far more serious was another marriage situation. As frequently happened a white man sincerely loved an Osage woman. Wanting to do the right thing for her, he would marry her legally under the white man's law. However, if he first neglected to marry her in a Me shin or O me ho marriage, the white man's wedding was deemed to be Ka shon le Me gro ka.

These marriage situations grew increasingly serious as the number of mixed bloods increased in proportion to the full bloods. Perhaps we should state the problem differently. As the proportion of Osages who did not live the traditional life grew in relation to those who lived the traditional life, a serious problem developed. The problem of determining who was Osage and who was not Osage could not be solved as long as two cultural bases were being used as the basis of determination. In the late 1800's it was decided to use only the English principle of *jus sanguine* or of the blood, as the measure of determining citizenship.[9] Adop-

[9]About 1897 the Tribal Council enacted a provision whereby Osage women with white husbands and children of such marriages were members of the Osage tribe. This was confirmed in the Act of 1906, Sec. 1. See Fifty-Ninth Congress, Sess. I, Chap. 3572, 1906.

tions was also retained in the Osage sense, that is, adoption is the same as blood. While this new yardstick did not cancel out traditional Osage marriages, it did make marriages of both cultures Me shin in effect.

Child Naming and Adoption

Child Naming

Introduction

Honorable men and women had to raise their children by tribal custom. Not only did the respect of others demand a child naming, but to become a member of the tribe a child had to be named. After the first three sons and the first three daughters had been ceremonially named, subsequent sons or daughters were considered to be ceremonially named. That is, the fourth son or fourth daughter was named without the full child naming ceremony.

Each of the first three sons and first three daughters had a special kinship term, which was used only within the family. Unfortunately, these kinship terms were sometimes recorded as names. As a general rule, each clan had a special name for each of the first three sons and daughters. In some limited cases these names were used by all kindred clans. Another limited exception was that a third son or daughter name in one clan may be a second son or daughter name in another. However, in general, the first three names were specific in order and unique to a specific clan. We will refer to these names as gentile names and other traditional names as clan names.

The sequence of kinship terms seem to be universal in all twenty-four clans. Only one variation is evident and that is in the use of the third daughter kinship term. The terms are as follows:

Sons	Daughters
First = E gro	First = Me nah
Second = Ka shon ka	Second = We ha
Third = Ka shin ka	Third = Se ka or Ah sen ka[10]

A family member would address a fourth son a Ka shin ka. Likewise, a fifth daughter would be called Se ka or Ah sen ka. All sons after the third son would be called by the third son kinship term. The same custom was applied to the daughters.

All of the gentile names and clan names were taken from the Osage myths. These names fall into two large groups. One group of names are called sky names; the other group of names are called earth names. This distinction is based on whether the name comes from a myth which tells of the life before the Little Ones came to the earth or after they came to the earth. If the name refers to the mythological sky events, it is a sky name. On the other hand, if it refers to the myths relating to the first days on earth, it is an earth name.

A man may have acquired a variety of names in his lifetime. Women rarely acquired additional names. Yet, a few women did become known by an honor name such as Ki he ka Wa ko or Woman Chief. Fewer yet, may acquire a trait name such as Wa ko Wa ke gre tsa ka or Crippled Woman. Men may take additional names through acts of bravery, offices held, achievements, or any number of events, as well as traits.

Child Naming Ceremony

Most Osage ceremonies have two or more versions depending on which clan is involved. The ritual given here is the Panther clan version. This is a peace rite and as such, references to war are omitted. When a family is ready to name their child, usually three

[10] Francis La Flesche, "The Osage Tribe: Two Versions of the Child-Naming Rite," *Smithsonian Institution, BAE, 43rd Annual Report,* (U.S. Government Printing Office: Washington, 1928), pp. 31-58.

to six months after birth, the clan Messenger is called. Each clan had a sub-clan that acted as Sho ka, Messenger, for its clan.

The child's father gives the Messenger a blanket as a fee for his services and a "little pipe" as a symbol of his errand. Then the father asks the Messenger to notify the Little Old Men of the Panther clan to assemble at the father's house. There, in his house, the father formally makes his wishes known. After this announcement, the heads of the two Peacemaker clans sends the Messenger to the other clans to have them assemble the next morning in the father's house.

Besides the Little Old Men of the Panther and Peacemaker clans there were Ancient Men of nine other clans to be assembled. These were: Hun ka Having Wings; Owners of the Black Bear; Elk; Fish People; White Osage; Little Male Deer; Elder Tsi shu; Elder Sun Carriers; and Buffalo Bull.

Before dawn of the next day the Ancient Men of the Panther clan gather at the lodge of the one among them whom the father appointed Ho ka or Prompter. The Assistant begins to recite the Ke non or Adornment Prayer. An aide paints the Prompter with red as the prayer is being recited. Next a downy eagle feather is fastened to his scalp lock. This represents the two sun's rays "first to appear," one ray for each division. These rays are symbolic of a never ending life. After the feather is in place, the Prompter is rubbed with buffalo fat which is symbolic of a plentiful food supply. Finally, a shell ornament, strung on a woven band, is hung from the Prompter's neck as the prayer ends. In the meantime, the other participants have gathered at the parent's lodge.

The next part of the rite is called Footstep Prayer. Both Houses of Mysteries must be approached with ceremony. In this rite, the "footsteps" are directed to the Peace, House of Mysteries. This "house" and all who enter it are a symbol of the universe and the myriad life forms in it. The child who is named in this house has the prayers of the participants for a long life and a perpetual line of descendants.

The Messenger leads the way to the House of Mysteries followed by the Prompter. They make four pauses on the way.

The Prompter sings a short song and recites one-fourth of the Footstep Prayer at each pause. They then enter the House of Mysteries and sit at the east end with the parents and child. All of the Little Old Men of the clans mentioned above also enter and take seats to the north or south according to their grand division.

When all the participants are seated, the Assistant proceeds with the Wa le le or Sending Ceremony. This is the sending of fees in the form of gifts to the headman of each participating clan. In return for the fees each headman recites the story of their clan's life symbol. This is done as soon as the sending is finished. They all recite at the same time, since this is not in unison or the same words, it seems very confusing at first.

At the conclusion of these prayers, a bowl of water and cedar fans, as well as a bowl of shelled corn, are placed before the Tsi shu Peacemaker headman. The Messenger then places the child in the headman's arms. After anointing the child with cedar water and touching the child's lips with corn, the child and bowls are passed to the Pon ka Peacemaker headman. He too anoints the child and touches its lips with corn. This tender ceremony continues from headman to headman until all have blessed the child in this manner. The ever flowing waters, the cedar, and corn are all symbols of a long productive life.

The mother is seated facing the Prompter with a buffalo robe, hair side down, between them. Red color has been placed at the head end, center, and tail, connected with a red line. (See Fig. 8.) In addition, the four legs are colored red. These represent dawn at the head end, midday at the center, and sunset at the tail end. The connecting line represents the sun's path.

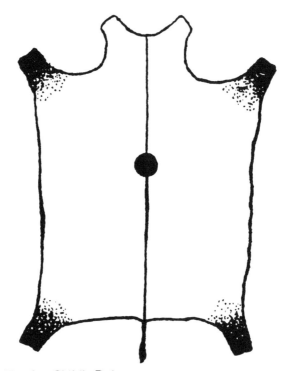

Fig. 8   Child's Robe
   (Drawn from an illustration in Smithsonian, BAE,
   43rd Annual Report.)

Instructions in food collecting and planting is now given to the mother. In collecting the lily root, the mother is instructed to use a staff made of willow. She is to dig the first root and place some of the mud clinging to it on her forehead then replant the root. This is symbolic of many descendants and the willow staff of a long life. The mother is also instructed to plant seven hills of corn. One seed in the first hill, two in the second and finally seven in the final hill. When the corn has milk in the kernels, it is to be harvested.

At this time of harvest, a feast is given for the Prompter and his friends. The main course is the sacred corn from the seven sacred hills. If a Prompter from the Buffalo Bull clan is present, he may recite the Corn Prayer of his clan. This feast signals the completion of the naming rite. Now the child has a place in its clan, in the sky, and on the earth, it is now united with the universe.[11]

Adoption

Introduction

As often happened, a war party would take a captive and bring him back to the village. Also, at times, a non-Osage would wish to become Osage. Since many families had lost a son or daughter there was always a place for adopted persons in the tribe. In an Osage adoption, the "new Osage" became as though he was born Osage by blood. In fact, adoption was considered to be a "new birth."

Adoption Ceremony

The headmen of the Tsi shu Peacemaker and Panther clans

[11]*Loc. cit.*

were invited to a feast at the adoptive parent's house. Ancient men from the Ice, Elk, Wind, Pon ka Peacemaker, and Hun ka clans were notified and assembled. The captive to be adopted was seated at the end of the house opposite the door. This was the traditional seat of the stranger and was on a raised platform. At this point, the ritual is the same as that used in child naming. After the ritual the grand Tsi shu chief leads the captive to the Panther headman. This act symbolized traveling the tribal circle through peace and war. Which is to say, the captive was to share as an equal in the good and bad of tribal life.

The Panther headman now took a keen flint knife and made a small cut at the tip of the captive's nose. Quickly, the grand Tsi shu chief wiped away the small amount of blood. Then the grand Hun ka chief brought water and the Hun ka headman brought buffalo meat and corn. The grand Tsi shu chief then placed the corn and meat against the captive's lips and gave him water to drink. A sacred pipe was filled with tobacco; cedar needles were placed on top by the Winds headman and then he lit the pipe. The captive smoked the pipe and was anointed with buffalo fat. Two black diagonal lines were painted from the left eyebrow to the lower right cheek of the captive.

When these things were finished, the grand Tsi shu chief would speak the words, Ne walla or Giver of Life, however, in this ceremony it meant, Made to Live. With these words the captive became the child of those who had adopted him. We must explain that while Ne walla is a name used by the Tsi shu Peacemaker clan, it was not a name bestowed on an adopted person.

In reviewing the ceremony, note of the symbolism should be taken. The letting of blood symbolized the loss of blood kinship to the people of the captive's birth. Wiping away the blood removed all trace of his former allegiance. Food and drink made new blood, since the food was Osage food the new blood was Osage blood. The smoking of the pipe also made the captive Osage in custom as did the anointing. Diagonal lines across the face symbolized thunder and the captive's duty as a tribal defender.

The adopted person was given a name from his new father's clan.[12]

Comments

We would like to make some comments in connection with adoption. The practice of adopting was mandatory under tribal laws, that is, a captive who wished to accept adoption could not be put to death. This was a common practice among the Siouan peoples. The willingness to adopt and absorb entire tribes of alien peoples is very evident among the Osage. A Siouan population explosion and rapid expansion westward seems to have occurred about the same time as the renaissance in Europe, 14th through 16th centuries. Although no detailed study of this phenomenon has been made, there has been a considerable amount of speculation.

The Osage myths, legends, and customs all tend to support the idea that much of the rapid population growth came from absorption of alien groups. Stimulation of thought processes seems to have come with the addition of new people. Examples are the Isolated Earth people who brought about the reorganization of warfare and Those Who Were Last to Come who brought the portable shrine concept. Valid arguments have been advanced to support the idea that the introduction of new people as well as moves to new environment tends to stimulate the thought processes of a culture.[13]

[12] Alice Fletcher and Francis La Flesche, "The Osage or Wazha' zhe, Tribe," *Smithsonian Institution, BAE, 27th Annual Report,* (Government Printing Office: Washington, 1911), pp. 61-62.

[13] Ellsworth Huntington, *Mainsprings of Civilization,* (Mentor Books: N.Y., 1959).

Education

Introduction

There was no formal education, as exists in the predominant culture today, in the Osage culture. Most education was by precept, but training in manual skills was by direct practice. Mental education was taught vicariously. These three approaches, precept, doing, and vicarious teaching, were effective in producing an educated people.

Osage life was well patterned and stable. The lines of expected conduct were clearly drawn as were the penalities for entering into forbidden practices. Precepts of right and wrong were everywhere held before young and old alike. Conduct was a common topic of conversation, and it was always noted how a respected person conducted himself.

Most Osage survival skills were physical skills. That is, they required coordination between mind and body. These skills were acquired by constant practice. The Osage used two types of bows, a long bow used when hunting afoot and a short bow used when on horseback. Each type of bow required a slightly different type of skill than the other. Constant challenges from older boys goaded younger boys to master the bows. The girls learned the corn grinding skills and the endless food preparation and preservation skills from their mothers.

Vicarious learning came mainly from the older generations. Each old man had a following of young boys. He would tell wonderful tales of adventure which the boys loved to hear. Almost all of these tales made a point of strategic or tactical cleverness in warfare or the hunt. With the reader's indulgence we would like to relate two of these stories. They were related to us, when we were young, by Sequoia Panther, a Cherokee-Quapaw.

Crow Butte

Deep in the Oglala country is a formation called Crow Butte. On one side is a sheer cliff and on the opposite side is a gradual incline. To the left and right sides a sheer scarp grows as one ascends the incline. About three-fourths of the way to the apex, the ramp narrows like the neck of an hour glass.

A young Crow needed horses for he wished to marry, and he was poor. Day after day he tried to find a way to acquire many horses. The lady of his heart was highly prized, so a great many were needed. One day he listened to an old Crow tell of a strange hill in the Sioux country. Suddenly, he knew what he had to do.

He gathered a small party of young men for the great adventure. For days they traveled deeper and deeper into Sioux country. At last they located the butte and camped at the base of the escarpment. The next day they built a huge smudge fire, hoping to attract the Oglala. By noon a large party of Sioux appeared. Taking only their weapons, the Crow ran to the ramp base. The Sioux dismounted and followed afoot. Step by step the Crow retreated up the butte until they passed the narrow causeway. There they were able to hold off the Sioux.

Deciding to let thirst and hunger weaken the trapped Crow, the Sioux settled down for the seige. Night fell and the fires of the opposing camps seemed to be omens of what would happen to the trapped Crow. So confident of victory were the Sioux that they did not even place guards on their horses.

At last, the sun arose and the Sioux had their breakfast. They talked of the Crow who had so foolishly allowed themselves to be trapped. After they finished their meal, two of the Sioux went to check on the horses. They returned in haste and reported that the horses were gone. A sense of disaster began to creep into the minds of the Sioux. They rushed across the causeway and found a rope, made of Crow blankets, dangling down the escarpment.

The Hunter

There was an old hunter who the young hunters had been teasing because he had not killed a single deer. The old man knew he had grown weak with age and unsteady in aim. Knowing this he made a stand at a salt lick. At last a deer came for salt. As he aimed, the old man saw movement on a rock above the lick. After careful scrutiny he saw a panther about to leap on the deer.

If he killed the panther he would lose the deer; if he shot the deer he would be at the mercy of the panther. Unable to decide, he waited, the panther killed the deer as the old hunter waited. On first impulse the old man was tempted to shoot the panther immediately. Being an experienced hunter, however, he trailed the panther as it drug the deer away. When they reached the panther's lair, the old man killed the panther. Four other freshly killed deer were already in the lair. The young hunters came up after hearing the shot. "See how a real hunter can kill five deer and a panther with one shot," exclaimed the old hunter.[14]

The lessons taught in these stories are obvious. Each old man had a collection of stories, many told to him when he was a child. Girls were also told tales that instructed and made the mental processes quicken. These were told by old women as they sat with busy hands. The patterns of these tales were invariably the same. An introduction giving the background, followed by rising action, then a minor climax and a surprise ending was the pattern. Almost always the ending had humor at the expense of someone's pride.

For the bright boys a special education was provided. The Little Old Men observed the young boys as they grew. They encouraged the devout bright boys by telling them stories about the Osage people. If the boy had an exploring mind, his questions were answered or he was shown the evidence so he could answer his own questions. Answers were not offered if questions were not asked. Thus, a mere retentive mind would learn rituals but not

[14] These stories were told to us by Sequoia Panther. However, they were also published in the *Osage Magazine*.

90

their meanings. An exploring mind would learn the rituals and their meanings.

A sincere bond of gentle feelings existed between the Ancient Men and their young students. Saucy Calf reveals this feeling while visiting with Francis La Flesche. With tears of memories he spoke of the Little Old Men who taught him. "... they were kind to me, those old men, when I was working hard to learn from them these sacred songs. As they sat around the fireplace I fed the fire to make it shed light and warmth and I ran to the spring to fetch water for them when they were thirsty. By these little services I won their affection and they were gentle and patient with me when they taught me."[15]

We still remember well the lessons taught by an old Osage. Day after day during a hot summer we sat in the shade and made quirts, whips, and ropes of rawhide. How patient he was with our untutored efforts. Carefully he would demonstrate each step and explain why it was done. At last the rawhide work was finished and we had a fine rawhide quirt. Then we learned how to make fiber rope. Many times we have recalled those summer days in the shade and that gentle patient man who perhaps taught us more than he realized.

It is a strange society we live in today. We separate the generations, the young do not know the old and the middle generations do not know the young or the old. We park our young wherever convenience dictates. Our aged are hidden in institutions and the middle generation is caught in a "rat race." No wonder the old Osages regarded farming and the white man's life as a trap from which there was no escape. To be educated one must have roots in the past, live in the present, and plan for the future. This is not possible with the segregated generations of today. The past is transmitted by the old to the young. The present is taught to the young by the middle generations. The future is the balance of past and present which the young create. As a society,

[15] Francis La Flesche, "The Osage Tribe: Rite of the Wa Xo Be," *Smithsonian Institution, BAE, 45th Annual Report,* (U.S. Government Printing Office: Washington, 1930), p. 534.

we would be wise to heed the wisdom of the Osage society and educate through the generations.

Parents

In an Osage family the parents were responsible for the education of their children. However, the mother alone taught both boys and girls for the first few years. At about five or six years of age the father took over the training of the boys. The girls remained pupils of their mother. An elder sister or paternal aunt may take over some of the instructional duties involving girls. If the girl was bright, the maternal uncle sometimes taught her some customs.[16]

The father may take his young son away from the village and show him how the coyote track has a peak in the middle while a dog track is domed in the middle. He must learn to judge how long it takes for the fine soil grains, around a track, to turn pale. Green leaves on the ground, broken twigs, cuds, and droppings must be the boy's open book. All running animals leave deep toe indentations and a comet-like tail or dirt grains behind the track, this too he must learn to read. Most of all he must learn to "see" from the "side of the eyes." A trick of vision prevents us from detecting small movements if we look directly at an object. These movements are easily seen in peripheral vision.

While the father exposes his sons to these things, it is the other boys who encourage the practice. Their games incorporated the skills they would need as men. The maternal uncle acted as advisor and mentor for the boys as they approached puberty. It was the uncle, who taught his nephew the finer points of tracking, hunting, and warfare.

Men, women, and children enjoyed the game of hand. Even the majority culture plays this game. It consists of concealing an object in one hand or the other and having someone guess which

[16] Betty R. Nett, "Osage Kinship System," *Southwestern Journal of Anthropology,* 8:175-176, 1952.

hand conceals the object. Reading face and body language was a highly developed skill among the Osage. They were equally adept at controlling their facial and body movements. This game was one of many used to refine these skills. In their dealings with the white man, they read the truth from these signs and not from the words he spoke.

Osage Mothers

Osage mothers were almost always devoted to their children's education. If one were to pick a single factor that made the Osages outstanding physically, mentally, and spiritually it would have to be the Osage mothers. Some idea of this devotion is given by John Hunter.

"Between the ages of two and three an infant boy is taken visiting with his mother. If he holds his own with infant boys his age she is happy and proud. However, if he withdraws from the conflict, she is sad and mortified. In the latter case the disappointed mother returns to her lodge and begins a program of special training.

She begins by placing a rod in his hand; assists him to beat and make flee the dog, or anything else that may come his way, and then encourages him to pursue. An adept in this, she teases and vexes him, creates an irritable temper, submits to the rod, and flees before him with great apparent dread. When skilled in this branch, she strikes him with her hand, pulls his hair, etc. which her now *hopeful* boy retaliates in a spiteful a *becoming* manner.

Some time having passed in this way, by which her pupil has learned to bear pain without dread, she takes him again on a visit, and I have never known an instance of a second disappointment in these trials of courage. They are then permitted to play with the other children of the village, and to quarrel and make up as well as they can.

After this conceived salutary course of discipline, the parents bring them back to their accustomed subjection, by a steady and determined course of government."[17]

In this practice we see a mother temporarily sacrificing her natural instincts to protect her baby because of the need to make

[17]Hunter, *op. cit.*, p. 272.

him courageous. These Osage women were made of steel, but at the same time they were devoted mothers. They were skillful and determined that their children would be achievers. It must be noted that Osage parents rarely used physical force on their children as punishment. The children were terribly pampered and spoiled. Yet, as adults, they were self-disciplined and amiable.

Bibliography

Burns, Louis F., *The Osage Annuity Rolls of 1878, First Roll, Second Roll, and Third Roll,* Ciga Press: Fallbrook, CA, 1980.

Fifty-Ninth Congress, Session I, Chapter 3572, 1906.

Fletcher, Alice and Francis La Flesche, "The Osage or Wazha' zhe, Tribe," *Smithsonian Institution, Bureau of American Ethnology, Twenty-Seventh Annual Report,* Government Printing Office: Washington, 1911.

Hunter, John D., *Manners and Customs of Several Indian Tribes,* Ross and Haines, Inc.: Minneapolis, MN, 1957, reprint of the original published in 1823.

Huntington, Ellsworth, *Mainsprings of Civilization,* Mentor Books: N.Y., 1959.

La Flesche, Francis, "Osage Marriage Customs,"*American Anthropologist,* ns, 14:1912.

———, Francis, "The Osage Tribe: Rite of the Chiefs; Sayings of the Ancient Men," *Smithsonian Institution, Bureau of American Ethnology, Thirty-Sixth Annual Report,* Government Printing Office: Washington, 1921.

———, Francis, "The Osage Tribe: Two Versions of the Child-Naming Rite," *Smithsonian Institution, Bureau of American Ethnology, Forty-Third Annual Report,* U.S. Government Printing Office: Washington, 1928.

———, Francis, "The Osage Tribe: Rite of the Wa Xo' Be," *Smithsonian Institution, Bureau of American Ethnology, Forty-Fifth Annual Report,* U.S. Government Printing Office: Washington, 1930.

Nett, Betty R., "Osage Kinship Systems," *Southwestern Journal of Anthropology,* 8:1952.

Panther, Sequoia, In the summer of 1939 Sequoia, then aged 72, and I worked together for the CCC, Indian Division. As we worked, he told me these and many other stories.

95

Watkins, Mrs. Rose Tinker, Personal visit with my maternal great aunt, *ca.* 1935.

CHAPTER V

Hunting, Planting, and Gathering

Hunting

Introduction

The Osages had three grand hunts a year unless a threat to their villages was impending. Two of these grand hunts were the spring and fall buffalo hunts. Almost every able bodied man, woman, and child in the village participated in these buffalo hunts. The remaining grand hunt was a winter hunt for deer and fur bearing animals.[1]

In addition to the grand hunts, many individuals and brothers made private or small hunts through the winter and early spring. The bear was hunted by small groups about a month after hibernation. Most small animals such as beaver, otter, bobcat, and raccoon were killed for their pelts rather than for food. A few of the old Osages said the bones of fish, fowl, and small game, "did not feel good in the mouth." Yet, others consumed these creatures with great relish. There is little doubt, however, that the "large animal" or buffalo, was the preferred food. The "small animal" or deer was next to the buffalo in preference. Third, in order, was "no sinews" or the bear.[2]

All of the grand hunts were ceremonially organized and conducted. Small hunts had no elaborate ceremony but prayers and songs were offered by the hunters. The ceremonies for the grand hunts followed the Wa ho pe or War Ceremony in almost

[1] William W. Graves, *The First Protestant Osage Missions, 1820-1837,* (The Carpenter Press: Oswego, KS, 1949), p. 13.

[2] Lewis Henry Morgan, *The Indian Journals, 1859-62,* (The University of Michigan Press: Ann Arbor, 1959), p. 82.

97

all facets. One must keep in mind that the welfare of the people depended on the grand hunts; it was a war for survival as was warfare against humans.

As soon as the ceremonies were completed in late May, the Osages left on the first grand hunt. A Director of the Hunt was selected in the ceremony as were eight soldiers or assistants. The actual hunt would be in charge of the Director and his Soldiers. While the people were going to and from the hunt the two grand division chiefs were in charge. The routes to be followed were determined by the chiefs.

Buffalo Trails

The first buffalo trail went from the villages in Vernon County, Missouri to a site north of present day Independence, Kansas on the Verdigris River. From there it passed north of Elgin, Kansas and southwest to the junction of Elm Creek and Salt Creek. This junction is west southwest of Cedarvale, Kansas. All four of the buffalo trails converged at this place. From the mouth of Elm Creek the trails crossed the Arkansas River a little upstream from Kaw City, Oklahoma. From there they went west to the Salt Fork and followed it to the Salt Plains.[3] While the Salt Plains were a favorite place for the base camp, the Osages frequently ranged much farther south, west, and north of this place.

At times they hunted south as far as the Washitas. They had pushed the Kiowa and Pawnee into this area. The Comanche of the Texas Panhandle, the Southern Cheyenne and Apache of the Plains in Southeastern Colorado also felt the Osage territorial push. To the north, as far as the Republican Fork, other tribes felt Osage hunting pressures. These areas, beyond the Salt Plains, were only partially controlled by the Osages. From the western

[3]Louis F. Burns, "Old Trails Across Northern Osage County," *The Chronicles of Oklahoma*, 59:422-429, Winter, 1981-82.

Salt Plains eastward to central Missouri and Arkansas, the Osages were supreme rulers.

The second buffalo trail ran from Black Dog I's village at the northeast edge of Baxter Springs, Kansas to the mouth of Elm Creek. This was a very special trail, because it was probably the first "improved road" in Kansas and Oklahoma. The second buffalo trail had several names. It is more commonly called The Black Dog Trail; at other times it was called the Manka Shonka Trail or Dog Who Cut with Axe Trail. It was completed and in use between 1800 and 1803.

Black Dog I and his band cut the trees and brush away to make the trail easier to use. Rocks were removed and stream banks were cut back to make the crossing easier. Campsites were marked and located at regular intervals. This trail which ran east and west was crossed by the north-south Osage Trace at present day Coffeyville, Kansas. The Osage Trace connected the Vernon County, Missouri villages with those near Claremore, Oklahoma. A northward extension of the Trace, connected the Vernon County villages with the villages at Ft. Osage on the Missouri River. Another trail connected the Vernon County villages with the Pomme Terre River villages and the village near Gravois Mills, Missouri.

From Coffeyville the Manka Shonka Trail followed the Kansas-Oklahoma state line to Caney, Kansas. West of Caney it turned southwest to the Hulah Dam on the Caney River. It followed the Caney River to the mouth of Buck Creek south of Elgin, Kansas. This campsite was called Gra to me shin ka or Little Hawk Woman. The trail then followed the north fork of Buck Creek and crossed the divide to the headwaters of Elm Creek. Following Elm Creek to the mouth, it joined the other trails at Salt Creek.

The third and fourth buffalo trails served the Osage villages on the lower Verdigris River. Claremore, Oklahoma was the center of the villages, but a small cluster of villages were about midway between Claremore and Coffeyville. This small cluster was served by the third buffalo trail which went slightly south of

Bartlesville, Oklahoma by Silver Lake to Sand Creek. The trail followed Sand Creek to northeast of Pawhuska and then crossed over to Bird Creek at Deep Ford. Finally, the fourth buffalo trail left Claremore and went west to Bird Creek which it followed to Deep Ford. From Deep Ford, now Pawhuska, Oklahoma, the third and fourth buffalo trails followed Bird Creek to its headwaters. There they crossed the divide to Elm Creek and merged with the other two trails.

An Osage custom is evident from these trails. Wherever possible the Osages followed stream courses. They traveled the high ground only when it was necessary to change valleys. Distances were always given in terms of the number of valleys crossed. In contrast, the white man traveled the high ground and only crossed rivers to reach other high ground. He always gave distances in terms of the number of ridges crossed.

When the U.S. Government forced the Osages to sell their Arkansas and Oklahoma lands to the Cherokee; the Cherokee wanted the second, third and fourth buffalo trails. These Osage trails and the lands beside them became known in history as the Cherokee Outlet. The Cherokee only used these trails once. They ventured out on the Great Plains away from the white man's forts, the hills and the trees. Here, the Osages and other Plains tribes inflicted such losses upon them that they never ventured to hunt buffalo on the Plains again. After the Osages repurchased the area between the Indian Meridian and the Arkansas River, the rest of the Outlet was opened for the Run of 1893. This run marks the closing of the American frontier. In many ways the Osage buffalo trails were the roads that led to the last frontier.

We do not want to leave the reader with the impression that these trails were a single track. Each of the four trails had alternate routes. At times, heavy rains required detours or protection from attack required a more sheltered route. Again, haste was a factor in selecting a route. These and many other factors influenced the decisions of the chiefs when they led their people to the grand hunt.

The Grand Buffalo Hunt

The grand Tsi shu chief led the people on the first day's journey. Very old people, the very young, and the infirm were left in the village. Departure and stopping times as well as the route was dictated by the Tsi shu chief on this first day. On the second day, the grand Hun ka chief led the people. The two chiefs continued to command on alternate days until the hunting party arrived at the place selected for the hunting camp. When the Osages traveled they observed two rules. First, they always camped on the side of a stream nearest to their destination. This was so a sudden flood would not delay them in the morning. Second, the doors of the camp wickiups faced in the direction of travel. When going west, the Tsi shu were to the south and the Hun ka to the north. This was the reverse of the normal order. Once they reached the base camps, the doors faced the normal direction, east. The Tsi shu were again to the north and the Hun ka were on the south. During war this same reversal of the normal order was also followed.[4]

Once the people reached the base camp, the Director of the Hunt and his Soldiers took charge of the hunt. Before they acquired horses the favored method of hunting the buffalo was by stampede. This method required the aid of everyone in the hunting party. They would approach the buffalo from downwind and frighten them into a stampede toward a gully or cutbank. Many buffalo would be killed or injured as the leaders tumbled over the edge. The living would be clubbed to death. Sometimes, a decoy would place himself near the edge of a gully. He would wear a buffalo robe, complete with the head, over his shoulders. As he "grazed," bent over, he would grunt like a contented buffalo would do. This led the main herd into thinking safety lay in that direction. As the herd rushed toward him the decoy would jump below the bank and run laterally to the oncoming herd.

[4]James Owen Dorsey, "Siouan Sociology," *Smithsonian Institution, BAE, 15th Annual Report,* (Government Printing Office: Washington, 1897), pp. 236-237.

Needless to say, the decoy was playing a hazardous role.

Another risky pre-horse method of hunting buffalo also used a complete buffalo robe. A bow powered arrow or stick propelled dart had a short killing range. Thus, a hunter must be very close to a buffalo in order to place his shot behind the ear or shoulder. With a robe draped over his bent body a hunter would "graze" upwind toward a cluster of buffalo grunting in contentment. When he got within easy range he fired his arrow from a crouched position. On this first shot he aimed for the lungs so the other buffalo would gather around their distressed companion. If luck was with him, the hunter could kill the whole cluster of buffalo. However, if they "winded" him he had a serious situation to solve.

The horse and the rifle made these ancient methods obsolete. By using the rifle from a "stand" and the same idea of the robe stalk, a hunter could safely kill a cluster and many more of the buffalo. Lung shooting an occasional buffalo caused the buffalo to gather around the wounded animal. Apparently the sound of a single shot at a time did not frighten them. William Cody, Buffalo Bill, used this method to supply meat for railroad construction crews. Several rifles were necessary since after a few shots they got too hot.

Hunting buffalo from horseback was exciting, dangerous, and not especially efficient. Osages preferred the bow and arrow over the rifle when hunting buffalo from a horse's back. They found the rifle to be awkward, dangerous, and unreliable for this type of hunting. Reloading was slow as well as difficult. Misfires were common because violent movement often spilled the prime from the pan. Since a running horse's back was an uncertain firing platform, a misaimed shot could easily wound or kill a fellow hunter if not the rifleman himself by an accidental discharge. Lances were sometimes used, but only to dispatch previously wounded animals.

Bows used from horseback were usually between three and four feet in length. In a cross section, they were slightly ovate. The preferred wood was Osage Orange,[5] but hickory was also sometimes used. The center or grip of the bow was often wrapped with wet rawhide strands which would shrink when dry and reinforce the bow. This shrinking was often so great as to leave indentations in the wood of the bow. Tendons were also used to wrap the center one-third of the bows. Bows used when afoot were usually longer than the English Longbow. In some examples we have seen, they were well over six feet in length. These were almost universally made of Osage Orange and were flat bows with no significant reinforcement in the mid section. Some of these foot bows had a series of small holes bored through the bow to the left and above the grip. Without a doubt these were peep sights for various ranges.

Other than the hunter, the most important factor in hunting buffalo from horseback was the horse. A buffalo horse was a very special Osage possession. These horses had to have more than speed and endurance, they had to be intelligent, nimble, and courageous as well. Since horses possessing all of these desirable traits were rare, one can understand why they were highly prized. When an Osage gave a gift of his buffalo horse, this was indeed a great gift. A buffalo horse was not ridden to the hunt; he was led. Only when the chase started was he mounted. Some of the finest "cutting" horses in the cattle industry were descendants of these buffalo horses.

There were dangers inherent to hunting buffalo on the Plains. The greatest danger was a possible attack from other tribes. At times the entire party of hunters would be assailed. More commonly, careless individual hunters were slain. First consideration was always given to protection and survival of the tribe. Individuals, by necessity, were a secondary consideration. Rules of the hunt, which were created by the Director and his Soldiers, sought to insure tribal and individual safety.

The Director of the Hunt had a difficult task. He not only had to insure safety but he also had to devise a fair and successful

[5]The French called the Osage Orange tree Bois d'Arc, but most Americans call it "bowdark" or hedge apple.

hunt. As in all human activities there were always laggards. Time must be allowed for the laggards to catch-up so all would have a fair start at the game. Sometimes, in the excitement of the chase a hunter went beyond the limits set for the chase. Such violators were punished severely by the Soldiers or other hunters detailed to mete out punishment. Arguments over the kill were settled by the Director. Hunters often marked their arrows so they could identify their kill. However, arguments sometimes occurred when two different arrows were in the same buffalo. The Director usually awarded the kill to the owner of the most fatal arrow. When the arrows were equally fatal, the kill was equally divided.

In the grand buffalo hunt, "All of the successive acts from the first choosing and sending out of runners to find a herd of sufficient size to supply all the people with food; the report of finding such a herd to the proper officials; the organization of a body of officers to enforce order when the hunters approach the herd; the sending forth of the tribal herald to give notice to the hunters to prepare for the chase; the approach of the hunters to the herd; all of these acts must be ceremonially conducted by the recognized tribal authorities."[6]

There were four ceremonial pauses as the hunters approached the herd. The Director and his Soldiers would sit on their horses side-by-side. Then they would smoke a ceremonial pipe as a prayer that the hunters would be protected from accidents, arguments that would disturb the peace, and bloodshed over dividing the kill. The hunters would be held back some distance so the ceremonies would not be interrupted.

Processing Hides and Meat

While Osages skinned buffalo from both the underside and the backside, the backside was preferred because it was easier.

[6] Francis La Flesche, "The Osage Tribe: Rite of the Wa Xo Be," *Smithsonian Institution, BAE, 45th Annual Report,* (U.S. Government Printing Office: Washington, 1930), pp. 561-562.

For ceremonial robes and other uses the animal was skinned from the underside. However, when meat was the major consideration the buffalo was skinned from the back. About 1830, they began to skin more and more from the underside, since the fur traders preferred hides skinned in this way.

The meat was brought back to the base camp for preserving. Osages rarely cut the flesh crosswise to the muscle. Bundles of muscle were stripped lengthwise and hung from racks to dry. In some cases the muscle may be cut crossgrain in a thin spiral so as to make an exceptionally long thin strip. These spiral strips and the longest "jerked" muscles were often braided, three strips to the rope, before being fully dried. After drying the meat was packed in parfleches, which were rawhide storage bags. [7]

The spring hides were not suitable for robes since the hair was loose. Hides taken in the fall hunt were best for robes and the hide trade because the hair was more firmly fixed to the hide. Spring hair was saved for use in weaving. Hides from the spring hunt were often utilized as wickiup covers, moccasins, and other uses where the hair was not especially important to its use.

Both spring and fall hides were stretched between stakes, hair side down. This was a task that required a considerable amount of skill since the hide shrunk as it dried. If the hide had been skinned from the underside, it must be stretched enough to even out the hump and yet not tear out the stake holes. When the hides were dry, they were "fleshed." That is, the bits of dried flesh still on the skin were removed. After these were removed, the flesh side was scraped to remove the paperlike membrane from the hides. These thin dry scapings were saved for later use as a coagulant on bleeding wounds. They were placed over the wound and were thought to assist in the healing process. Another use for these scapings was as the base for a waterproofing glue which was applied to parfleches.

We would not want to leave the impression that hair on spring

[7] Francis La Flesche, "The Osage Tribe: The Rite of Vigil," *Smithsonian Institution, BAE, 39th Annual Report*, (Government Printing Office: Washington, 1925), p. 203.

hides was so loose that it all fell out of the hide. Most animals shed their winter coats with the coming of warm weather. Therefore, the hairs become loose in their sockets and come out easily. This causes the buffalo to "itch," so, lacking trees to rub against, they would tear the sod with their horns and roll in the roughened sod. This action created what was commonly called buffalo wallows. As the colder fall weather approached, animals begin to grow a new winter coat. The hair follicles contract and the hair is held tightly in the hide during cold weather. Thus, fall and winter hides became prime material for robes and bedding.

Osages used rawhide and tanned hides, some were used with the hair still on them, others had the hair removed. To remove all the hair from a buffalo hide three methods were used. The ash-lye method had two variations, one was to boil the hide in a water and wood ash solution. Another was to place moist ashes over the hair side and place moist soil on top of the ashes. In both cases the ash-lye loosened the hair and made it easier to scrape off. For hides to be used in making parfleshes, the hair was hammered off with a hand size rounded stream stone. To do this the flesh side was placed on matted grass and the hide was struck a slanting blow on the hair side. This action cut off a clump of hair, with repeated blows the entire hide could be freed of almost all the hair. In the process the rawhide was made more pliable and easier to work. Buffalo hides to be tanned were most commonly covered with buffalo dung on both sides and kept moist for three to five days. Deer skins were more commonly soaked in acorn tannin. After the tannin in the dung had penetrated throughout the hide, it was cleaned and rubbed with buffalo brains. The brain oil was worked into the hide and the fibers loosened by a variety of ways. A favored way was to drive a stake into the ground and dome off the top. With this in place, the hide was drawn back and forth over the rounded stake until the hide was pliable. Another method was to lay the hide over a log and beat it with a bat sized stick. Doeskin was sometimes chewed to make it pliable, then it was rubbed with powdered calcite. The tanned hides were often smoked and stored high in the lodge where smoke frequently lingered. Rawhide ropes were the kind most widely used by the Osages. However, the highly prized horse hair and buffalo hair ropes were superior in "elastic" qualities. Some of the "hair" ropes were three strand twisted ropes. The six and eight strand plaited horsehair ropes were the best the Osages had and would rival the nylon lariats of today. Rawhide ropes were, by far, the easiest to make.

A hide taken from a young cow was preferred for a rawhide rope. The hide must be skinned from the underside and dehaired. Stomach, neck, and joint hide areas are not suitable for rope making. Hide from these areas separate into many loosely adhering layers and is referred to as "sorry" leather. The back and side hide is shaped into an oval. Starting at the outside edge of the oval a thong about three sixteenth of an inch or a quarter inch wide is cut. By cutting only the outer edge, a thong 120 to 150 feet long will be cut before the center of the oval is reached. This thong is then cut in half. Each half is looped back from the middle to make four equal strands. Both loops are hooked over a stub twig to hold them while plaiting. This makes a four ply rope thirty-five to forty feet long. To keep the rawhide soft and pliable while cutting and plaiting, it must be periodically soaked in water. After the work is finished the rope is allowed to dry. This "seats" the plaiting firmly because of the shrinking.

The Winter Hunt

The fall hunt ended in early October. By mid November, the third grand hunt was under way. This hunt was conducted from the main villages. The game was primarily deer or the "little animal." Since deer are sensitive to sounds and sights, large groups of individuals would be easily sighted and heard. For this reason the larger group broke-up into groups of three or four hunters. These small groups radiated out in all directions from the village. Some two or three valleys away from the village they would make "stands" and wait for the deer.[8]

[8]*Ibid.*, pp. 308-322.

At times, these small groups would hunt bear. Bears were in hibernation by November, but they were in excellent flesh since they had only recently hibernated. The hunters would light torches and go into the caves. When they found a bear they would slay it. Hibernating bears were partially awake at this time, so they were easily roused. Bear hunting in caves, even during hibernation, was risky, to say the least.

Planting

Introduction

It has been said that seven kinds of corn and seven kinds of squash fell from the heels of the first buffalo. Certainly, the buffalo was considered to be a food animal.[9] Corn was considered to be a food plant. Both were treated as gifts from the Mysterious Giver of Life. In addition to corn and squash, which was sometimes called pumpkin, the Osages also raised beans which were called peas. These beans or peas were grayish white with brown spots on them. They tasted very much like cow peas and pinto beans.

Women owned the fields and crops. All work done in the fields was performed by women or under their direction. Sometimes men and boys assisted with the heavier work, but always under the direction of the woman who owned the field. In Osage minds, a special relationship existed among the woman, the earth, and the seeds she planted.[10]

Women brought new human life into the visible world which they nourished and tended until that new life could stand alone. In planting seeds, she also brought new life from the darkness into the visible world. She tended the plants and brought them to maturity. Thus, through woman, both mankind and plants were

[9]*Ibid.*, p. 207.

[10]La Flesche, *45th Ann. Rpt., op. cit.,* pp. 623-629.

able to have an endless line of descendants. Possibly this was a device to push the planting task upon women, yet, the parallel between the life giving powers of the earth and women could not be ignored. In any event, the area planted was not large enough to entail extensive labor.

A fairly accurate estimate of one-third of an acre per person has been made.[11] This would include all crops raised. Probably two acres per family cultivated by two or three women would be a close average. Considering that men assisted in clearing vegetative debris and weeds were hoed only once, the labor expended by women was not prohibitive. We do not mean it was not hard work, it was. What we are saying is, women were not slaves to their fields.

The ground was cleared about mid March and corn was planted. Corn hills were spaced two or three feet apart. In mid May the corn was "laid-by" or given the final tilling. Most of the people then left on the spring buffalo hunt. When they returned in late July some of the corn would be in the "milk" stage. That is, it could be eaten as roasting ears. The ears were roasted in the husk by digging a pit for the ears and covering them with about three-quarters of an inch of soil. Four to six inches of live coals were then placed in the pit. When done, buffalo fat or bone marrow was spread on the ears which were eaten hot. Steam roasted this way, roasting ears took on some of the husk flavor and was far more tasty than boiled roasting ears.

Processing, Storage, and Use

Surplus roasting ears were husked and silked. They were then boiled briefly to stop the enzyme action. The kernels were removed from the cob and spread out to dry. After they were thoroughly dried, they were placed in loosely woven sacks and hung high up inside the lodge. Added to meat stock stew, the dried corn gave to the stew a greater savor. Dried corn was also added

[11]Robert H. Lowie, *Indians of the Plains*, (The Natural History Press: Garden City, NY, 1954), p. 23.

to pemmican or eaten as a side dish.

As soon as the roasting ears were harvested, pumpkins were planted between the corn hills; a few beans were planted in the same manner. After a short rest, preparations were made for the fall buffalo hunt. The period following the fall hunt was one of busy activity. Mature corn, pumpkins, and beans had to be harvested and stored. Beans were shelled and stored like dried corn. The husks of mature corn were pulled back and tied in strings. These strings of corn on the cob were also stored high in the lodge. Pumpkins were cut in strips and partially dried, then the strips were braided and completely dried. The braids were stored in parfleshes hung inside the lodge.

Mature corn was used in variety of ways. Some of it was shelled, parched, and soaked in lye-ash water. After about forty-eight hours, the corn was washed repeatedly in clear water. The outer skin would easily slip away in the washing. Boiling with bear side meat, bear bacon, made a dish of what is commonly called hominy. Mature corn was also ground into a meal which was added as a thickener in stews. Sometimes the meal was mixed with acorn flour to make a cake called "squaw bread." Today this "fry bread" is made with wheaten flour. The old style "squaw bread" was eaten with maple syrup. As the white man drew nearer, bees provided honey.[12] Today sorghum is often eaten with "fry bread."

While it was customary to store foodstuff and hides in the lodge, the amount of supplies made it impossible for everything to be stored there. Secret caches of supplies were also maintained. These caches were usually in well drained areas. Customarily they were dug in the shape of a jug. That is, they had a narrow neck leading from the surface which widened as the cache deepened. The floor and circular wall was lined with sticks. When filled, a hide was placed at the bottom of the neck and then the neck was filled with dirt. Horses were often driven over the cache

[12]Honey bees were not native to North America. When bees appeared, the Indians knew the American settlements would follow within two or three years. In a sense, the bee was the vanguard of the American Frontier.

to hide the location in the hoof prints. At other times a fire was built over the cache to disguise the difference in the soil.

In some cases these caches were cut into solid rock. Black Dog had his people dig a cave which was used for storage and a hide out. In the Cherokee attack on Claremore's village, Place of the Oaks, near Gra moie's Mound, Black Dog's people at Big Cedar, now Claremore, Oklahoma, were saved by this concealed cave. We must explain that all the able bodied Osages were away on a buffalo hunt, otherwise, the Cherokee would have never dared to attack.

Corn Ceremonies

So important to the Osages was corn, that it had many places in the ceremonies. Indeed, several songs are devoted to corn planting alone. One of these is the Wa le ha Ke non or Adornment for Raking. Another was the U she Wa lo or Planting Song. Adornment for Raking refers to the symbolic painting before clearing the field. The woman paints the part of her hair red. This was put on before sunrise and removed after sundown. It was done for four successive days.[13]

During the U she Wa lo or Planting Song the Messenger gives to the selected women a woven sack and a planting pole.

"Each woman throws upon her back the bag, drawing the carrying strap around her shoulders, and stands with the pole in her right hand. The woman is the planter, the cultivator, the harvester of the corn, and this little scene is meant to portray the important part she plays in the drama of life. As the season for planting draws near she clears the field of dead stalks and weeds, mellows the earth with her crude hoe, and then builds the little hills that stand with their faces looking upward to the sun to receive its animating rays. When all the little hills have been made, she begins her planting by thrusting a sharpened pole into the center of the sunny side of a hill, and into the hill thus made five, six, or seven grains of corn. Then she performs the last act, which is regarded as the most significant and sacred; she places upon the mound over the hole,

[13]La Flesche, *39th Ann. Rpt., op. cit.,* p. 284.

111

the imprint of her foot. It must be her right or her left foot, according to the tribal division to which she belongs."[14]

Gathering

Introduction

A great variety of uncultivated products grew in the Osage homeland. Aside from the foodstuffs, a large quantity of vegetable and mineral materials were gathered. Wood was widely used for fuel, tools, and ornaments. Beads were cut from fresh water mussel shells. While most of these shells were white, a few were pale blue, and very rarely a beautiful pink. Fossilized bracipods were also used for beads; the calcite took both vegetable and mineral dyes very well.

Minerals

Silicates, such as flint and chert, were collected in large quantities. Other silicates such as quartz, agate, and obsidian were sometimes acquired by trade. Since flint and chert were so widely used by the Osages, we will explain somethings about them. Chemically, flint and chert are the same, however, chert is white or pale in color while flint has true color. Both are found as concretions in limestone beds. This happened because high silica clay masses were deposited with the limestone. Southwestern Missouri has extensive deposits of red and pink flint as well as white to cream chert. Black Dog's band used rose flint almost exclusively, some of this came from Southwest Missouri and some from a hilltop south of Cedarvale, Kansas. Most of the flint in the Flint Hills of Kansas has been weathered out from no longer existing limestone beds. These flints are usually a smooth brown on the outside and cream to tan on the inside.

[14]Francis La Flesche, "The Osage Tribe: Rite of the Chiefs; Sayings of the Ancient Men," *Smithsonian Institution, BAE, 36th Annual Report,* (Government Printing Office: Washington, 1921), pp. 294-295.

Some sizable pieces of flint, weathered smooth brown on the exterior, are found in shale banks in northern Osage County, Oklahoma. Most of this flint is gray-black with white fossils in it. Some crude artifacts have been found made of this material. Other pieces are a smooth grained striped buff color. This is an excellent flint and was widely used.

All of the silicates, including windowglass, have a spalling characteristic which enables a craftsman to shape them with simple tools. If pressure is exerted on a small edge area with a deer horn, the flint will flake off on the underside in a halfmoon flake. By "nibbling" at the edges and pushing sidewise on high spots it is possible to shape the silicates. Needless to say, some Osages were more adept than others at working flint. This difference in skill shows in the artifacts. On some the flat surfaces are so smooth the spalls can barely be seen and the edges are a razor sharp series of minute points.

Other minerals were gathered for various uses. Yellow, green, and red clays were gathered for paints. Native copper was hammered into ornaments. Black catlinite was preferred for pipes. Some clay was used in fired pottery. Coal and its properties were known to the Osages, but they had no regular use for it. Large deposits of selenite were in the tertiary beds of the Southern Great Plains. The primary use for selenite and its kindred minerals gypsum and calcite was to whiten doeskin. West of the Salt Plains are the Gypsum Hills which furnished an abundant supply for all the Osages used.

Sandstone was widely used to fine grind corn, as sharpening stones, and as sanding tools. Since the hand grinding stones once were abundant at old campsites while the stationary mate was rarely found, we assume the grinding was mainly done on large nearby rocks. Many of these so-called hand grinding stones were probably used to hammer the hair from buffalo hides rather than to grind grain. We have never had the pleasure of investigating the site of a permanent Osage village so we cannot comment on the use of large stones for grinding. The large stones around the hunting camps we are well acquainted with do not show signs of grinding. It does not seem logical that grain would be ground traveling to and from the buffalo hunts. We are inclined to believe these hand stones were used for dehairing buffalo hides.

Fig. 9. An Arrowshaft Polishing Block

A few arrow shaft polishers made of sandstone are sometimes found. (See Fig. 9.) These are small blocks of sandstone about three-eighths to one-half inch thick, an inch wide and two or three inches long. They have a "U" shaped groove running lengthwise down the center of the one inch width and for the entire length of the block. Truing and polishing arrow shafts were their primary functions although the reverse sides of some show they were used to sharpen knives also.

It does seem strange that novaculite is never found at the Osage campsites. The finest deposit of this silicate discovered to date is in the Missouri homeland of the Osages. In view of the fact that novaculite is the best natural honing stone known to the world, it is difficult to understand why the Osages did not use it for any purpose.

Vegetative Material

Vegetative material, other than wood, was also gathered in large quantities. Bark was used for house covering. The cambric layer of some trees was used as a coagulant for bleeding wounds. Baskets, mats and bags were made of cattail rushes, buckbrush roots, and nettle plant. Cattail rushes were widely used for woven mats and bags. The nettle plant was sometimes used in the warp and cattail rushes in the woof of some articles. Baskets were

114

sometimes made from the buckbrush roots. Cedar gum was gathered and used as a glue.

Medicinal Herbs

Herbs of many kinds were gathered for the treatment of ills. The widespread stereotype of a witch doctor casting spells and dancing around an ill Osage is not even partially true. Among the old Osages, an understanding of what could and could not be done for an affliction was well known. Beyond treatment of wounds, surgery was unknown. Broken bones were not reset and internal surgery would have horrified them. Yet, they had a good comprehension of internal medicine. For example, they too felt bleeding was sometimes beneficial, but they were more moderate in its use than European doctors of the 1800's. To give some idea of the herbs and uses of Osage medicine a few examples are listed here.

Tu te se ha, It Expels the Wind
anise roots were frequently eaten when traveling. It was thought
   this would help rid the body of gas.

He ne pe scah, Fire Gone Out
ashes were used to make lye. In a very much diluted form this was
   used for sour stomach. Corn soaked in lye water was also used
   for this ailment. Tobacco and mountain laurel ash was used to
   treat ulcers.

Hun ko ka O ka sha, It Stops the Blood Flowing Out
astringent root or poppy mallow roots was used to stop the bleeding from wounds. The dried root was powdered and applied as
   a poultice. Internally, a half teaspoon in cold water is a dose
   for bleeding. It was also used as a wash when a woman
   menstruated.

She scah ne shu, Washing in the River
bathing was a preventative. Most Osages bathed daily.

Wa sop pe he ka, Fat of the Bear
bear oil was used both internally and externally with many herbs.
    For colds, anise or wild licorice was seethed in bear oil and
    drunk as hot as possible. Buckeye leaves were mixed with bear
    oil and put on the skin as a mosquito repellant.

He ne scah, Dark Colored Liquid
black walnut hulls readily color water a deep brownish black.
    Taken in one ounce doses, and repeated at intervals, it was
    believed to relieve colic.

Ta tun ka O pa, Eye Ball of the Buck
buckeye nut was used for diarrhea. Special caution, the buckeye
    nut and leaves are deadly poison. Symptoms are contraction of
    the neck muscles, crossed eyes, body bloat, severe constipa-
    tion, and almost total loss of muscular action. Convulsions
    immediately before death is common. A dosage of two grains
    are a maximum. Ten grains are equal to three grains of opium
    in effect. Like opium, buckeye is a narcotic.

O ka she ka, Running on the Ground
dewberry root was used in cold water for bowel complaint. How-
    ever, it was not felt to be very effective.

Shen do Shu tsy, Bitter Red Berry
dogwood bark was used for fever. It was also effective as a
    poultice for sores such as boils.

E ha sho ka, Bites the Mouth
Indian turnip (Jack in the Pulpit) was used for coughs and
    malaria. For coughs it was given in a tea combined with spike-
    nard and wild anise. As a malaria treatment, it was taken when
    the fever was off, combined with snake root and wild cherry
    bark.

Ne pe she, Bad to Touch

milk weed roots were used as a tea for dysentery, dropsy, and asthma. It was also used as an emetic.

Ka nic ka nic, Mixed Tobacco

sumac leaves and roots were used. Both leaves and roots were thought to be especially good for dropsy. A half and half mixture of sumac leaves and tobacco was considered to be a fine smoking mixture.

Ne ne shu ka ah, Salt Water Flows

sweating was a widely used remedy. This was sometimes brought about by drinking large amounts of warm water. Another method was to bundle up in skins or robes. By far the most popular means was a sweat house. This was a small wickiup built over a fire pit containing stones. Water was poured on the heated stones which generated steam. The steam induced profuse perspiration. In some cases a person would run from the sweat lodge and plunge into cold water. In others, they would go home and bundle up.

No ne aw, Tobacco

tobacco was used as a hot moist mixture to draw local inflamation to a "head." Moist tobacco was also used to draw venom from stings and spider bites.[15]

Firewood

Gathering firewood became an increasingly difficult task as a village site aged. This meant the women had to go farther each year for wood. However, most villages were near to rivers and floods often deposited driftwood in the willows which grew on gravel bars. These driftwood piles usually teemed with snakes so

[15]John D. Hunter, *Manners and Customs of Several Indian Tribes,* (Ross and Haines, Inc.: Minneapolis, MN, 1957), pp. 369-395.

117

the women had to be cautious. Very little wood was cut or split. In Europe, this type of wood was called faggots, in America it was called squaw wood.

It takes little imagination to see that wood for fuel was highly prized. Recognition of this was given in the ceremonies. In the Pa tse U ke or Contributed to the Fire Ceremony, the seizure of wood from four warriors is to remind them of their duty to protect the deer from intruders. A stick of firewood would then be taken without asking for permission from a member of each clan. Only the two Peacemaker clans were exempted as an act of reverence. The wives of the men last initiated into the tattooing rite were also exempted. However, if the collector insisted on taking the wood the woman had the right to demand that the collectors recount their war honors. If they could not do this, then they could not have the wood. Only those who had defended the women and children could take wood for ceremonial purposes.[16]

Wild Food Plants

An abundance of wild foodstuffs were available in the Osage homeland. These were the first to be protected from the intrusion of uninvited people.[17] While the buffalo supplied the bulk of their diet and the deer was next in order, the corn, pumpkins, beans, and wild foods added variety to the diet. All of these together were kept in a state of delicate balance. When the people could not go on the buffalo hunt, the balance was upset. This placed an inordinate demand upon the supplies of deer and wild plants. Intruders, brought about the same upset in balance. Without the buffalo meat, the deer and native plants were depleted almost to the point of extinction.

[16]Francis La Flesche, "War Ceremony and Peace Ceremony of the Osage Indians," *Smithsonian Institution, BAE, Bulletin 101,* (U.S. Government Printing Office: Washington, 1939), pp. 47-48.

[17]La Flesche, *36th Ann. Rpt., op. cit.,* p. 185.

118

Recorded history shows an unvarying pattern of missed buffalo hunts preceding each land cession. This is true of the Treaties of 1809, 1825, and 1868 as well as the Act of 1870. Intrusions during the Wakarusa War in Kansas and the subsequent American Civil War had exhausted the native natural food supply. By 1875, hide hunters had left only a few stragglers of the Southern Buffalo Herd. Even these were gone after 1878. Thus, the Osage were forced to rely on deer and natural food plants. These supplies were all but exhausted by 1906. A radical revolution in Osage life was the result.

The Osage homeland was rich in nuts such as walnuts, hazelnuts, pecans, and acorns, especially the chinkapins. Other fruits which grew wild were grapes, plums, black haw, dewberries, blackberries, strawberries, papaws, and persimmon. Roots and bulbs were also gathered, the main ones were wild onion, water lily, groundnut or wild bean, saggitaria latifolia or arrowhead plant, and falcata comosa which is a vine bearing pods above and below the ground.

Walnuts were collected and the soft outer hull was tromped loose, then they were allowed to dry. Pecans were flailed with poles and picked up from the ground; hickory nuts and hazelnuts were harvested in much the same way. The chinkapin acorn, walnuts, pecans and hickory nuts could be eaten without roasting or boiling. Other acorns such as burr oak, red oak, black jack, and post oak contained too much tannin to be eaten raw. Roasting removed most of the tannin and the large burr oak acorn was especially good when roasted. Tannin was sometimes removed from the red oak acorn by boiling. The liquid was used in tanning deerskins and the "slush" was used as flour after drying.

Grapes grew profusely on the valley floors. There was the common wild grape which was smaller than the fox grape which was also sweeter than the common grape. Two varieties of plums were found. The hill or ridge plum was about marble sized and on the sour side, but the sand plums were larger and also sweet in taste. Black haw was almost entirely seed, while the flavor was excellent, it was hardly worth the effort to separate the seed from the pulp. Dewberries and blackberries were nearly identical, the dewberries came earlier in the year and were larger than the blackberry. Wild strawberries were about half the size of cultivated strawberries. However, they were sweet and rich in flavor. These were often found on east facing slopes where the dead fall grass made a deep mat.

Papaws were a fall fruit which grew on small bush-like trees in river bends. They had a rich almost overwhelming banana flavor. Papaws resembled the common banana or plantain of The South Pacific in shape. That is, they were rounded at both ends rather than being pointed like commercial bananas bought at the market. They also grew singly rather than in bunches. The skin was yellow with brown blotches. Once the thin peel was removed the pulp was soft.

Persimmons grew in small groves of slender tall trees with bark similar to black jack oak except it was finer grained. While they preferred to grow on valley floors, they also flourished on gently sloping hillsides. The bright orange fruit was slightly smaller than a golf ball. This fruit was very astringent and would "pucker" the mouth if eaten before the first fall frost. When fully ripe, the fruit became wrinkled and had dark blotches on it.[18]

Osages would gather this fruit and screen the seeds from the pulp. These screens were made from rodlike saplings laid side by side. The pulp would be forced between the rods thus removing the seeds. Next, the pulp was patted flat on a paddle-like board and baked over live coals. Then they were sun dried before being stored in a parflesh. Some say they tasted like chocolate cake, but to us they tasted more like gingerbread. The Osage name for the persimmon is Sta en ka and the preservation of this valuable Osage food is called Sta en ka Ka he.[19]

Wild onions grew in heavy black soil that was soggy in the spring. Large earthworms, about as large as a pencil, were always

[18] Graves, *op. cit.,* p. 12.

[19] *Smithsonian Institution, BAE, Miscellaneous Collections,* no. 10, 76: 104-107, 1923.

found in association with wild onions. The onions were almost identical to small tender commercial scallions. They were frequently the first new green to appear in the spring. Because of this, milk cows would often eat the tops in the spring which gave the milk an unpleasant taste. Wild onions were eaten raw; the green tops and white bulb were both consumed. They were also added to stews and broths to add zest to winter weary palates.

Water lilies have the scientific name of *nelumbo lutea*. However, they are also known as "water chinkapins," and the Osage name is Tse walla. The roots and nuts of this water plant were the principal source of food among the wild plants. Ox-bow lakes were often near Osage villages and campsites. Both the water lily and cattails flourished in these shallow still waters. Women would wade among the lily pads and probe in the mud with a pole. When they located a root with the pole, they dug it out. The roots were long and armlike. As soon as possible after digging, the outer skin was scraped away. After scraping, the root was cut into one or two inch pieces which were strung on thongs and hung in the sun to dry. Both the nut and root were eaten raw when fresh. Roots were also cooked when fresh. Nuts and roots were stored in large quantities for future use.

Apios apios is the botanical name for the wild bean. It is a member of the pea family and was also known as the groundnut plant. *Sagittaria latfolia* is a water plant, like the lily, characterized by arrowhead shaped leaves. *Falcata comosa* is a vine with trifoliate leaves and small white or violet flowers. Pods are found above and below the ground. These three plants furnished some of the Osage diet, but not nearly to the extent furnished by the lily.

Cookery

Osage cookery with meats produced tasty meals. Roasting was most commonly used, and two methods were employed. One involved wrapping the meat in leaves and covering it with first ashes, then a bed of live coals. The other method was to suspend the meat by a vine over the fire; a variation was to place the meat on a slanted stick at the fire's edge. Broiling was accomplished by fanning the ash from a bed of embers and placing the meat directly on the coals. Next to roasting the most widely used cooking method was by stewing and boiling. Before the white man came, a pit was dug and lined with moist clay about an inch thick. After building a fire in the pit, to temper the clay, the pit was cleaned and filled with water. Hot stones were dropped in the water to boil food. Shards found at campsites indicate they also made and used pottery pots for this purpose. Corn of all kinds, lily roots, bone marrow, fat and meat were all added to the pot.[20]

The first metal trade kettles were made of sheet copper or brass. We have some indication that these became unsatisfactory to the Osages at an early date, possibly because of copper chloride poisoning. In an account about the Osages killing all the Kiowas in a village they beheaded the dead and put the heads in new brass pots they found in the village.[21] As a warning to other tribes, heads were normally stuck on sharpened stakes. The Kiowa, Comanche, Pawnee, Cheyenne, and Apache usually called the Osage "head cutters." In the finger talk or sign language of the Plains, the sign for Osage is a chopping motion with both hands at the nape of the neck. It does not seem likely the Osages would have left new brass pots if they placed a high value on them. The Osage were among the first buffalo tribes to receive the cast iron kettles. Although these iron kettles were much heavier than the sheet copper and brass kettles, they were more durable and safer to use.

John Hunter mentions an Osage custom that was unknown to us. "Every individual supplies himself or is supplied with a separate dish and eating utensils, which are used on all ordinary occasions, and even taken to their feasts by them, and they are never exchanged or used by any, except the rightful owners."[22]

[20]La Flesche, *39th Ann. Rpt., op. cit.,* pp. 129-130.

[21]George E. Tinker and C.J. Phillips, editors, "The Osage: Historical Sketch by the Editors," *The Osage Magazine,* 1:23, Feb., 1910.

[22]Hunter, *op. cit.,* pp. 267-268.

Bibliography

Burns, Louis F., "Old Trails Across Northern Osage County," *The Chronicles of Oklahoma,* 59: 1981-82, Winter.

Dorsey, J. Owen, "Siouan Sociology," *Smithsonian Institution, Bureau of American Ethnology, Fifteenth Annual Report,* Government Printing Office: Washington, 1897.

Graves, William W., *The First Protestant Osage Missions, 1820-1837,* The Carpenter Press: Oswego, KS, 1949.

Hunter, John D., *Manners and Customs of Several Indian Tribes,* Ross and Haines, Inc.: Minneapolis, MN, 1957, reprint of the original published in 1823.

La Flesche, Francis, "The Osage Tribe: Rite of the Chiefs; Sayings of the Ancient Men," *Smithsonian Institution, Bureau of American Ethnology, Thirty-Sixth Annual Report,* Government Printing Office: Washington, 1921.

_____, Francis, "The Osage Tribe: The Rite of Vigil," *Smithsonian Institution, Bureau of American Ethnology, Thirty-Ninth Annual Report,* Government Printing Office: Washington, 1925.

_____, Francis, "The Osage Tribe: Rite of the Wa Xo' Be," *Smithsonian Institution, Bureau of American Ethnology, Forty-Fifth Annual Report,* U.S. Government Printing Office: Washington, 1930.

_____, Francis, "War Ceremony and Peace Ceremony of the Osage Indians, *Smithsonian Institution, Bureau of American Ethnology, Bulletin 101,* U.S. Government Printing Office: Washington, 1939.

Lowie, Robert H., *Indians of the Plains,* The Natural History Press: Garden City, NY, 1954.

Morgan, Lewis Henry, *The Indian Journals, 1859-62,* The University of Michigan Press: Ann Arbor, 1959.

Smithsonian Institution, Bureau of American Ethnology, Miscellaneous Collections, no. 10, 76:1923.

Tinker, George E. and C.J. Phillips, editors, "The Osage: Historical Sketch by the Editors," *The Osage Magazine,* 1:1910, Feb.

CHAPTER VI

War

Introduction

There has been a tendency on the part of writers to stress the warlike attributes of the American Indian. This should be expected since the histories of Western Civilization places heavy emphasis on wars. Warfare is without a doubt more exciting than the mundane activities of daily life. The effects of war are dramatic and revolutionary; the effects of peace are prosaic and evolutionary. Achievements forged in the hell of war are more often than not, transitory. Those born of peace tend to be solid and lasting. Since they are evolutionary the changes are too slow to be dramatic.

The Little Old Men were aware of this aspect of human survival. Peace was stressed as an ideal, symbolized by a cloudless day and the white swan. Yet, these Old Men were very much realists. They realized men resorted to violence more readily than to gentleness. For this reason they encouraged defensive warfare over aggressive warfare. This thinking extended to the war honors. The highest honors were for defense of the village, women, and children. In short, for defending the survival of the tribe. Very few of the war honors required the taking of human life. Striking a blow against an enemy was sufficient in most honors.[1]

Like other humans, the Osage often committed terrible acts in the heated emotions of conflict. To judge these acts by standards of an alien culture is an act of ignorance. Many acts of the Western Civilization horrified the Osage. Yet, these same acts were considered to be acts of civilized men. The rape of the earth

[1] Francis La Flesche, "The Osage Tribe: Rite of the Chiefs; Sayings of the Ancient Men," *Smithsonian Institution, BAE, 36th Annual Report,* (Government Printing Office: Washington, 1921), pp. 248-249.

is only one example. It was difficult for an Osage to understand why the white man beat his own children is another example. They were appalled at the wholesale slaughter of men at war in "civilized" wars as a final example.

While there were examples of wholesale slaughter by the Osages, these were still exceptions rather than the general practice. Some acts, such as placing heads on stakes, were indeed, brutal but effective warnings. Slaughter more commonly occurred when "bluff warfare" had failed or in retaliation for like action. While there was no honor in killing a coward, the Osages killed such persons in contempt. A person of courage had the respect of the Osages and stood a better chance of survival.

To most white men, Indians had no rules of warfare. Yet, the mountain men and others who lived among Indians tell us otherwise. Among themselves Indian tribes fought each other often but as often became friends and allies. They understood each other. When the immigrant tribes, such as the Cherokee, invaded Osage territory they used the white man as an unwitting ally. This practice was alien to the buffalo tribes. Eventually, many of the buffalo tribes allied with their traditional enemy, the Osages. They understood the Osages, but they did not understand the immigrant tribes.

An Osage custom which was often erroneously called the war ceremony, was actually a burial ceremony. A mourning party would go out to slay a single enemy. The scalp of an enemy would be brought back to complete the ceremony. This was done in the belief that the enemy would accompany the deceased Osage over the lonely spirit path to spirit land. Only outstanding warriors or their families were so honored. In later years, only a bit of hair was clipped leaving the "victim" unharmed.

Organization of a War Party

The leader of a war party was called To tun hun ka or Sacred One of the War Party. Although he accompanied the war party he

126

did not direct the party or participate in the fighting. His function was spiritual. He was the first to be appointed by the Little Old Men. The other officers were not appointed until the Sacred Leader completed his seven day vigil. Going to and from the battle he traveled and camped apart from the war party. This was so he could concentrate on prayers to Wa kon ta. To the religious Osage, his was the most important function. Hence, he was considered to be the leader in Osage minds, if not in the minds of Western Civilization.

To Western minds, the actual leaders were the next two officers selected. The majority culture has become so accustomed to the concept of one supreme leader, that they sometimes forget there are some advantages to two or more supreme leaders. Those masters of military organization, the Romans, operated for some time under a triumvirate. Americans conceive unity to be following one leader. The Osages conceived unity as a consensus of the two grand divisions; Tsi shu or sky and Hun ka or earth. Thus, one leader from each division, working together, was a united leadership. If one seeks a further advantage, they should note, that, the Osages were never plagued with "strong men on horseback." This expression is used to describe a situation where a strong military leader seizes the government by violent revolution. The United States is one of the few countries in world history to escape this affliction. Like the Osages, the Constitution keeps the military subordinate to the civil government. However, the Osages went a step further and divided military authority as well as civil authority.

The two officers selected to be the actual leaders of an Osage war party were called Wa sop pe ah le Wa sho wa gra. One was taken from the Tsi shu grand division and the other was taken from the Hun ka grand division. Next appointed were eight officers who were called Hra tsa ka, which is in archaic Osage, and the meaning has been lost. Four of these officers were appointed from each grand division. They were under the direct command of the actual leader of their division. These eight officers form a council and determine details such as routes,

127

campsites, and commands to the warriors.

Volunteers for the final class of officers were asked to stand. The first man of each clan to stand was appointed leader of the warriors from his clan. These clan officers were called Tsa ha ke. His first task was to recruit men of his clan for the war party. In a way, these clan leaders were comparable to platoon sergeants. Since they were the officers who carried the Hawk Wa ho pe into battle, they were the ones who led the charge. A war party would have a maximum of twenty-four Wa ho pe officers. Ordinarily each of the twenty-four clans would muster from ten to thirty warriors for a large war party. Such a war party would be around a thousand men. At their greatest size the Osages probably could have fielded between seven and eight thousand warriors.[2]

The Symbolic Man

When Tecumseh, the great Shawnee Chief, spoke to the Osages in Vernon County, Missouri, they likened him to their Symbolic Man. To the Osages he was everything an ideal Osage man should be. He possessed an ideal body which was tall, flat muscled, and well proportioned; in addition, he was dark in complexion and had thin but strong long-fingered hands. His voice was deep and melodious, which with his keen intellect and graceful gestures made him a great orator. In describing Tecumseh, as the Osages saw him, we have described how the Osages pictured their Symbolic Man.

Normally the Symbolic Man stood facing the east. The north or left side of his body represented the Tsi shu who occupied the left or north half of the village. The right or south side of his body represented the Hun ka, who, in peacetime, occupied the south half of the village. These positions were normal in peacetime, but in war the positions were altered.

[2] Francis La Flesche, "War Ceremony and Peace Ceremony of the Osage Indians," *Smithsonian Institution, BAE, Bulletin 101,* (U.S. Government Printing Office: Washington, 1939), pp. 13-20.

As soon as the two leaders, the Wa sop pe ah le Wa sho wa gra, were appointed, the Symbolic Man reversed his position and faced the west. The entire village was also reversed with the Tsi shu to the south and the Hun ka to the north. This movement was symbolic of the tribal unity as the Symbolic Man was also symbolic of tribal unity in peace as well as war. Only with peace would the village return to the normal order.[3]

War Paint

There were at least three styles of Osage war painting. All three required painting with sacred charcoal. When the entire face was blackened with charcoal, it meant an all out no quarter battle. A blackened upper face and yellow lower face indicated a "bluff war." While this may seem to be an advantage to an enemy, one must bear in mind when the Osage wore black paint, death was certainly a probability. Osage mourning parties customarily wore red paint from the ears on down on both front and back. Alternate red and black stripes were painted on the face. This clearly meant someone was going to die.

Charcoal made from the redbud tree was the first choice of the Osage. However, charcoal made of willow could be substituted if necessary. This charcoal had to be ceremonially created to be sacred. Charcoal itself was a symbol of fire. Fire was considered to be both a destructive and beneficial force. In war, it was a symbol of total destruction. Its application by a warrior was a vow that he would show no mercy to the enemy.[4]

Strategies and Tactics

Strategies were battle plans made before the attack and

[3] Francis La Flesche, "The Symbolic Man of the Osage Tribe," *Art and Archaeology*, 9:68-72, Jan.-Jul., 1920.

[4] John D. Hunter, *Manners and Customs of Several Indian Tribes*, (Ross and Haines, Inc.: Minneapolis, MN, 1957), p. 345.

tactics were plans made once the battle started. Osage strategies were developed on the basis of observation. Going to and from a battle they kept scouts deployed around the party. Customarily, they avoided the skyline and always sought trees or rocks, when crossing a ridge, to avoid being skylined. The number of advance scouts was increased as the signs indicated they were nearing the enemy. These scouts relayed information back to the officers. Based on the data received, the officers formulated a strategy. The favored strategy was an all out, frontal, no reserve assault. Terrain and placement of the enemy sometimes favored a feint attack from either or both flanks followed by a carefully timed frontal attack. On the Plains, they often used a "decoy and draw" strategy. A decoy party would allow themselves to be "surprised" by the enemy force. They would flee in evident panic drawing the enemy into an ambush prepared by the main party.

It must be noted that the Osages and Indians in general lacked some important elements of strategy. First, the reserve concept was not known to them. By this we mean, they did not hold back a reserve of warriors who could be used to bolster unforeseen weaknesses that often show once the fighting starts. Next, they lacked the important support facilities such as food, water, and munition supply. Their strategies never extended beyond a single battle. Finally, they lacked a variety of specialized units. For example, a unit of armored lancers to protect a unit of bowmen.

Lacking these elements, Osage warfare was primarily tactical. European writers often commented, that, once Indians won a victory in a single battle they did not capitalize on the victory. That is, they did not hit the enemy again and again until he was unable to fight any more. This is basically true, however, it should be noted that over several generations the Osages nearly annihilated the Wichita, Pawnee, and Kiowa. They did this while at the same time they held the Sac and Fox to the area north of the Missouri River and the Muscogee tribes east of the Mississippi. In this same century and a half they held the French and Spanish to a narrow shelf on the west bank of the Mississippi.

The only force, known to us, that accomplished a similar feat against such odds was Lee's Army of Northern Virginia. Only when Grant deprived Lee of his tactical superiority in the last one hundred days of the Civil War was Lee defeated. Grant placed his strategically superior reserves and supplies against Lee's tactical superiority by maintaining constant contact. Unable to manuever and resupply Lee was worn down by Grant's numerically larger force. Although Lee inflicted losses that were close to five to one against Grant in battle after battle, Lee lost the war because he could not replace the men he lost and Grant could.

To the white man, the Osage and other Indians seemed foolish when they did not make better use of their victories. Given the military limitations of no reserves and no resupply in the field, they would have been foolish if they had maintained a prolonged warfare. The Viet Nam War was a classical example of tactical warfare waged against a strategically superior force. We could point to the Russian forces in Afghanistan or innumerable other examples. However, the lesson seems to be clear, Osage type of tactical warfare is extremely effective unless it is subjected to constant contact by a strategically superior force.

While one may, with logic in their favor, argue that hit and retreat is actually a strategy, it is pure tactics that make it successful. The art of tactics lies in knowing when the maximum damage to the enemy has been inflicted with the minimum loss to the attacker. This is the "break-off point" of a battle; if the battle continues the attacker's losses will be greater than his gain. The Osages seemed to be especially adept in sensing this point. More importantly, they had the ability to withdraw their warriors from the heat of battle like shadows in the night. At times, they would reform their forces and strike the enemy from another quarter before the foe could get organized for a pursuit. When pursued on the Plains a common tactic was to set fire to the grasses. Pursuing enemy forces had a great need to advance with caution, since the Osages often set-up ambushes and traps, such as deadfalls and rockslides. This possibility slowed the pursuit which increased the chances of a safe retreat for the Osages.

The Osages preferred to go to war on foot, even after they first acquired horses. The Southern Great Plains tribes called them "the walkers" when referring to this habit of the Osages. There were at least two advantages to this practice. Men on foot could conceal themselves better on the Plains than men on horseback. If the warriors knew they faced a long hazardous walk home if they failed to win the battle, they would fight harder. On the other hand, if they should win, they could ride home in comfort. Another advantage was the matter of leaving tracks and signs of the presence of a striking force. A horse left clear tracks, urine, and excretement. Moccasin tracks were faint and control of elimination signs could be enforced. This lessened the possibility of a surprise attack on the war party.[5]

Valor Adornments

Like most Indians and the white man, the Osages used adornments to symbolize their victories. An adornment worn only by warriors was a deer tail headdress dyed red.[6] This was fastened to his scalplock and stood up like a roach. A distinguished warrior also wore a small, rawhide, round shield on his back. This shield was painted with symbols of his achievements and ringed with fluttering eagle feathers. Scalps were not always taken, but a count of those slain was kept. When a warrior reached To pa or four slain, he painted a blue half circle, points downward, on his breast.

The crow was much respected by the Osages. He was always associated with battles, because he followed men on the warpath. After a battle the crows were pictured as approaching the slain warriors two by two or in pairs of two. There they tore at and ate

[5] George E. Tinker and C.J. Phillips, editors, "The Osage: Historical Sketch by the Editors," *The Osage Magazine,* 1:23, Feb., 1910.

[6] Francis La Flesche, "The Osage Tribe: The Rite of Vigil," *Smithsonian Institution, BAE, 39th Annual Report,* (Government Printing Office: Washington, 1925), pp. 274-275.

the flesh of the fallen warriors. At times they would flutter into the air when fighting over a special morsel. When finished, they would fly away two by two as they came. Like the crow, the wolf was also esteemed by the Osages. He was the symbol of the eight commanders because of his endurance and keen senses of hearing and scent.[7]

Some of the Osage warriors were presented, ceremonially, a special honor. This was a badge worn on the hips, which was called Ka he or crow. A crow skin, wolf tail and two pendants of eagle feathers were attached to the badge. The badge is a symbolization of the battle scene. Crows and wolves were symbols of war and the pendants represented the fluttering crows after the battle. A similar honor among the Dakota Sioux is called a crow belt.[8]

Distinguished war leaders were often tattooed if they could afford the fees. If they were especially prosperous, their wives were also tattooed. Male and female tattoos were different designs except for the spider on the back of the hands. These tattoos were dark blue although charcoal and kettle black was used as the coloring material. Three implements about the size of new pencil were used in tattooing. These have a row of needles at one end and a rattle made of pelican quills at the other end. Originally, splintered wing bones of the pelican were used as needles. Tail feathers of the woodpecker were used to apply the coloring and to outline the design.

The male tattoos are all symbols of war. These are: (1) The sacred ceremonial knife; (2) the sacred pipe; (3) the thirteen sun rays. (See Fig. 10.) Running vertically from under the chin to the abdomen is the sacred knife. Slanting from the knife point, on each side, and then over the shoulders, is the sacred pipes. Representations of the thirteen sun's rays are two diagonal designs which also run from the knife point and over the shoulders.

[7]*Ibid.*, p. 124.

[8]*Ibid.*, pp. 127-128.

133

Tattoos placed upon a woman's body were more extensive and intricate than those worn by men. It was an act of love for a warrior to have his wife and relatives tattooed. A woman was considered equal in importance to the warrior, for upon her rested the

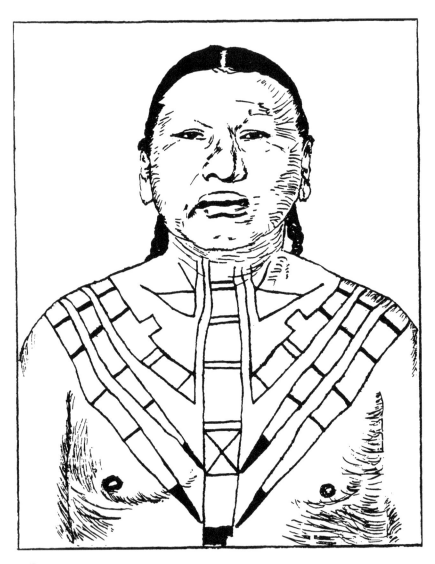

Fig. 10 A Tattooed Osage Man
(Drawn from a picture in Smithsonian, BAE, Misc. Coll., vol. 63, no. 8.)

134

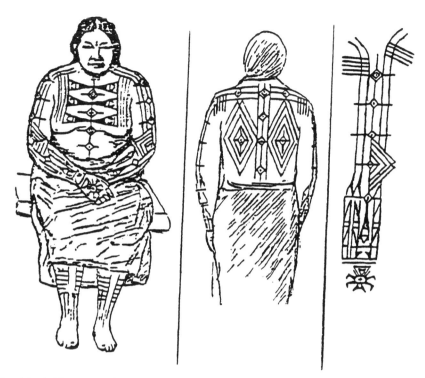

Fig. 11. A Tattooed Osage Woman
(Drawn from an illustration in Smithsonian, BAE, Misc. Coll., vol. 70, no. 2.)

tribal existence. (See Fig. 11.) She had two small circles tattoed, one over the other, centered between the eyebrows. Her chest, back, arms, hands, and lower legs were tattooed with geometric designs. These were stylizations of the sun, moon, stars, and the earth from which all life originated. Running from her shoulder and down her arm to the wrist were symbols representing life in all forms descending to earth. The spider, like the Ho e ka, represents a snare or trap which holds life on earth until released by death.[9]

[9]*Smithsonian Institution, BAE, Miscellaneous Collections,* no. 2, 70: 111-113, 1918.

War Honors

Although all the divisions had thirteen war honors or O ton, they used different symbols when counting them. The Tsi shu grand division used the thirteen sun rays of the rising sun. Between the two Hun ka subdivisions, earth and water, each used different symbols. The earth or Hun ka sub-division used thirteen footprints of the Black Bear. Wa sha she or the water sub-division used thirteen willow trees as their symbol.

War honors were always given in a group of seven first and then in a group of six. The group of seven represented the left or Tsi shu side and the six represented the right or Hun ka side of the tribe. Customarily, when giving their war honors, ceremonially, willow sticks were used to keep count. These were referred to as "this" in the ceremony and at the end of each honor the stick was dropped on the Wa ho pe or Hawk Portable Shrine. We have listed below the thirteen war honors of Saucy Calf as he would have recounted them in a ceremony.

"I rise to count my war honors. It is at your request, O, Wa sha she, Hun ka, and Men of Mystery, that I rise to recount my war honors. You well know that the war honors that have been awarded me are not altogether clear of doubt, but it is your wish that I recount them on this occasion, and I cannot but give consent to your request."[10]

The Seven War Honors

(1) This represents the war honor known as O skon scah tse Ka sa ke, Striking the Enemy within the Camp Limits. A Pawnee warrior was slain within the camp limits on Salt Creek. To tun e no he was first to strike the warrior, and being next to him in the attack I gave the enemy the second stroke, which entitles me to a like war honor. O, thou Wa ho pe that lies before me, I place this upon thee.

[10]This comment is a conventional plea of modesty.

136

(2) This represents the war honor called Wa lu ha pa.[11] I won it in a fight by a grand war party, composed of both the grand divisions of the tribe. The sacred charcoal was still upon my body and face when I performed this act and there exists no doubt of my title to count this war honor. O, thou Wa ho pe that lies before me, I place this upon thee.

(3) This represents the war honor known as To tun he tun ka Wa tsa gra, Triumph of a Leader of a Grand War Party. Ne ka ka hre came to me in his bereavement and, weeping, asked me to go forth to slay an enemy because of his loss. I went forth and came back in triumph. O, thou Wa ho pe that lies before me, I place this upon thee.

(4) This represents the war honor called Wa tsa, Victory. I won the war honor when, as the officer carrying one of the standards of a war party, I struck an enemy. O, thou Wa ho pe that lies before me, I place this upon thee.

(5) This represents the war honor To tun ke tun ka Wa ka hre, Striking an Enemy in an Attack by a Grand War Party. I won this war honor when under the leadership of Me ka Shin ka, a war party attacked and slew a member of the enemy. O, thou Wa ho pe that lies before me, I place this upon thee.

(6) This represents the war honor called Moh shon tse Ka hre, The Striking of an Enemy in the Open Country. I won this war honor by striking a single enemy attacked at break of day by a war party of which I was a member. O, thou Wa ho pe that lies before me, I place this upon thee.

(7) This represents the war honor called Tse Ka ha tun ka Pa Wa lu sa, Taking a Head in an Attack by a War Party Composed of Warriors of Only One of the Two Grand Divisions. I won this war honor in an attack made by a war party led by Wa kon ta u ke a. O, thou Wa ho pe that lies before me, I place this upon thee.

[11] This refers to dropping an unused captive strap on the body of a slain foe.

The Six War Honors

(1) This represents the war honor called Wa ho pe U kon tse Wa lu ha pa, Striking an Enemy While a Member of a War Party Only One Wa ho pe. I won this war honor in an attack made upon the enemy by a war party led by Ku she wa tsa. O, thou Wa ho pe that lies before me, I place this upon thee.

(2) This represents the war honor called Wa ho pe U kon tse Wa tsa gra, Successful Leader of a War Party Carrying Only One Wa ho pe. I won this war honor as leader of a war party carrying a single Wa ho pe. O, thou Wa ho pe that lies before me, I place this upon thee.

(3) This represents the war honor called Wa ho pe U kon tse Wa ka hre, Striking an Enemy in an Attack Made by a War Party Carrying Only One Wa ho pe. I won this war honor in an attack made by a war party led by Gra moh shin ka. O, thou Wa ho pe that lies before me, I place this upon thee.

(4) This represents the war honor called Moh shon tse U tse, Striking an Enemy in an Attack in the Open Country. I won this war honor in an attack made by a war party led by Tsa to ah moie. O, thou Wa ho pe that lies before me, I place this upon thee.

(5) This represents the war honor called Tse ka ha Wa tsa gre, Successful Leader of a War Party Composed of Warriors of Only One of the Two Grand Divisions. I won this war honor as the successful leader of a war party. O, thou Wa hope that lies before me, I place this upon thee.

(6) This represents the war honor called Wa ho pe U kon tse Pa Wa lu sa, Taking a Head of an Enemy in an Attack Made by a War Party Carrying a Single Wa ho pe. I won this war honor in an attack made by a war party carrying but one Wa ho pe. O, thou Wa ho pe that lies before me, I place this upon thee.[12]

[12]La Flesche, *39th Ann. Rpt., op. cit.,* pp. 179-181.

While all of these war honors were important, the single most important was the first named. U skon scah e ka sa ke or A Blow Given to an Enemy Within the Limits of the Village is the name of this highest honor. Opportunities to earn this honor both because the village and fields were well guarded and because of another limitation were rare. This honor could only be earned within a year after a member of the Black Bear clan was initiated into the Rite of Vigil. The time started after the ceremony when the Little Old Men of the Black Bear clan issued the decree. In the ancient days there were few initiations into the Rite of Vigil so this was a severe limitation.[13]

Wa shin Le le Ke non

This is literally, painting to send the will. No Osage warrior went into battle without being aware that he carried his own courage and the courage of his loved ones. We are not qualified to state whether the Osages could send their courage by will power or not. Perhaps, when current studies in ESP are completed, answers will be forthcoming. More importantly, the Osages believed they could send courage by will power. Confidence in this power gave added heart to warriors on the warpath. When the Osages went to war every Osage went to war either in body or in spirit.

Women who had brothers away at war went through this ceremony of sending the will. Before sunrise on the day after the warriors departed she would paint the part of her hair red. This represented the sun's path and made it difficult for death to overtake her. A short vertical blue line was placed on the cheek of her division, left if Tsi shu and right if Hun ka. She would then put her lodge in order. On the next sunrise she would repeat the painting but a red vertical line would be placed beside the first blue line.

[13]*Ibid.,* pp. 67-68.

This continued for four consecutive sun rises and days. On the third day a blue line would be placed beside the red line. Finally, a red line would be placed beside the second blue line.[14]

[14]*Ibid.*, pp. 284-285.

Bibliography

Hunter, John D., *Manners and Customs of Several Indian Tribes,* Ross and Haines, Inc.: Minneapolis, MN, 1957, reprint of the original published in 1823.

La Flesche, Francis, "The Symbolic Man of the Osage Tribe," *Art and Archaeology,* 9:1920, Jan.-Jul.

————, Francis, "The Osage Tribe: Rite of the Chiefs; Sayings of the Ancient Men," *Smithsonian Institution, Bureau of American Ethnology, Thirty-Sixth Annual Report,* Government Printing Office: Washington, 1921.

————, Francis, "The Osage Tribe: The Rite of Vigil," *Smithsonian Institution, Bureau of American Ethnology, Thirty-Ninth Annual Report,* Government Printing Office: Washington, 1925.

————, Francis, "War Ceremony and Peace Ceremony of the Osage Indians," *Smithsonian Institution, Bureau of American Ethnology, Bulletin 101,* U.S. Government Printing Office: Washington, 1939.

Tinker, George E. and C.J. Phillips, editors, "The Osages: Historical Sketch by the Editors," *The Osage Magazine,* 1:1910, Feb.

CHAPTER VII

Mourning

Introduction

White men often confused the Mourning Rite with the Wa sop pe Ah le or War Rite with good reason. The two ceremonies were almost identical. Most of the Ancient Men who left a recorded view on the question of which was first to be used, say the Mourning Rite came later in time than the War Rite. The original rite was for the purpose of organizing a war party for offensive or defensive warfare. Organizing a mourning party was for the purpose of obtaining a spirit to travel the spirit path with the spirit of a deceased Osage. There was a belief that the path to spirit land was a lonesome journey. Believing the departed Osage wanted company on the trek, the Osages sent another spirit to accompany the deceased Osage.[1]

Origin of Mourning War

A story about how this custom originated has been handed down through the generations. Long ago an honored man lost a relative and went into a mourning fast. He wandered across many valleys in order to be alone with his grief. Suddenly, the winds brought the voice of the deceased relative to him. The voice asked him to send the spirit of an enemy so they could go to spirit land together. At once, the mourner returned to the village and organized a small war party. The war party slew several enemy. With a scalp in hand, the mourner returned and fastened the scalp

[1] Francis La Flesche, "War Ceremony and Peace Ceremony of the Osage Indians," *Smithsonian Institution, BAE, Bulletin 101,* (U.S. Government Printing Office: Washington, 1939), pp. 86-87.

143

to a pole planted at the relative's grave. Other people followed this practice except they organized the war party ceremonially. In this manner, the custom of sending an enemy spirit to accompany the spirit of a deceased Osage originated.[2]

Among the more difficult things for a mourner to do was to sincerely mourn for the enemy slain, so his spirit could accompany the spirit of a deceased Osage. Respect for all life required that the slain enemy must also be mourned. Especially since his life had been ended before its allotted time on earth. One can understand how easy it is to mourn for a loved one and how difficult it is to mourn for an enemy. This act required a very difficult mental feat. To be less than sincere in mourning for the slain enemy would be a mockery of the entire ceremony. So, for seven days the mourner fasted and sincerely mourned for the enemy he had killed.[3]

Mourning Ceremony for Fallen Warriors

There were two ceremonies for sending away the spirit of a warrior slain in battle. The first was conducted by his companions-in-arms after the battle and the other was conducted by the entire tribe. On the fourth day after the battle the Leader of the war party announced that the spirit of the slain warrior was still with them and demanded to be released. An especially beautiful tree was selected to represent the sun. The Leader reached as high as he could on the trunk and cut a strip of bark to the base. After he had cut four strips, one for each of the four winds, each member of the party would cut a strip the same way or until all the bark on the lower trunk was removed. Then the entire party would face the sunrise and hold their palms toward the sun. After this, they would paint the exposed wood red and release their slain warrior's spirit to join the rising sun.

When the war party reached the limits of the village, they

[2]*Ibid.*, p. 87.

[3]*Ibid.*, pp. 138-139.

would form a circle and start to wail. Sounds of the wailing would soon reach the village, the people would then assemble around the circle of wailing warriors. A Little Old Man of the Elk clan and another of the Winds clan would hastily put on their paint. They would make four pauses to recite prayers as they approached the circle. On arriving at the circle of warriors they would enter the circle.

As in the creation myth, the Elk clan man would call for the four winds. Responding to the appeal, the Four Winds man would come with a pouch of cedar needles. It is said, that thunder and the four winds dwell in the cedars. The four winds are the symbol of the breath of life and the voice of spirits. Ceremonial pipe and fire lighting is an office of the Four Winds clan. A fire was lighted and the Four Winds man would drop a pinch of cedar needles, from his pouch, on the fire. This was done for each of the four winds. A cedar torch was then lit and carried around to the warriors who breathed the smoke emitted from the torch. This act freed their bodies from the touch of death. Breathing the smoke cleansed their bodies of the spirit of the dead.

After the cleansing of their bodies, the warriors would remove their clothing and place them in a pile with their weapons. Horses complete with the equipment used in the battle were also brought into the circle. When all articles used by the war party had been assembled, they too were exposed to the cedar smoke. After this cleansing, all of these things became the property of the two Ancient Men who performed the ceremony. A final act was a procession of Little Old Men from the Four Winds clan. They would walk around the borders of the entire village. It has been said, the spirit of the dead could not cross this path. The warriors, dressed in new clothing could now enter the village.[4]

Reasonable efforts were made to discourage the taking of another human life. In the ceremonies a part called the Weeping Songs support this statement. As the Weeping Songs were about to start, the Prompter would speak to the people assembled for the

[4]*Ibid.*, pp. 139-141.

ceremony. "Oh! brethern, it has been said that if anyone has any compassion for me at the performance of this part of the ceremony he will rise." In the Osage manner of ceremonial expression, the Prompter is asking those in mourning to abandon plans to seek another life. He is reminding them that such a practice can bring them no comfort and will only bring death and sorrow to others.

When the singing started, most of those in mourning willingly rose and wept the final tears for their departed loved ones. With the end of this ceremony, they discarded the ragged clothing and blankets they wore in mourning. They cut their hair again and wore paint and washed away the soil of mourning. Once again they were at peace in their hearts and wept no more.[5]

Adornment for Burial

A person who had been initiated into the Rite of Vigil or the Rite of the Wa ho pe degrees was given a special painting at death. First, the entire body was painted red. Then, with dark paint, a vertical line was drawn on both cheeks from the forehead hair line to a line even with the mouth. A horizontal line, just below the hairline, was drawn across the forehead to connect the vertical lines. This line represented the horizon of the earth and with the vertical lines formed the Ho e ka or snare, which drew all life into the trap. The Ho e ka is also a symbol of the earth. Four vertical lines were then drawn from the horizontal line to a point a little above the eyebrows. These lines represented the four winds which was symbolism for the breath of life and the voice of spirits. On the right side near the last rib, the dark figure of a man was drawn. This figure represented the spirit of the deceased person.[6]

[5]*Ibid.*, pp. 232-233.

[6]Francis La Flesche, "The Osage Tribe: The Rite of Vigil," *Smithsonian Institution, BAE, 39th Annual Report,* (Government Printing Office: Washington, 1925), p. 73.

Changes

Conditions had so changed by the early 1900's that the mourning ceremony as practiced in the early 1800's was hardly recognizable. Yet, the basic elements were still intact. Certainly, the taking of scalps had been discontinued since May of 1873 with the furor over killing a Wichita Chief.[7] Deer had been substituted for a human victim. Most of the clan organization was gone although much of the dramatic representations were still retained. So few of the Little Old Men were left after 1900 that a full muster for the old ceremonies could not be gathered. At least one and possibly more of the clans had no living representatives. Possibly, the ceremonies were coming under the influence of the American Indian Peyote religion of the Southwestern tribes.[8]

However, old customs, long in use, do not entirely yield to change. Even today Osages proud of their heritage cling to the remnants of the customs practiced by their forefathers. In a world so different than the world that gave birth to the customs, perhaps the spirit of observation is more important than the manner of observation.

Burial

We know of three Osage graves over one hundred years old. These graves are still intact and one could look at them and still not see them. All of these graves are on the south point of hills or at the foot of south facing cliffs. We were told by one who helped bury these Osages, that their bodies were placed in a sitting position facing east. Once in place, rocks were placed around the bodies leaving only a small "window". These three graves, before

[7] La Flesche, *Bull. 101, op. cit.,* pp. 141-142.

[8] George A. Dorsey, "The Osage Mourning-War Ceremony," *American Anthropologist,* ns, no. 3, 4:404-411, Jul.-Sep., 1902.

the village was moved, were completely disguised to keep white people from digging them up.

Early settleres in Vernon County, Missouri noted numerous mounds of Osage graves on a high hill near the main Osage villages. In these, too, the bodies faced east in a sitting position although the graves were on top of the hill. Stones were piled in mounds around the bodies. Some accounts relate that when a descendant or friend passed by, they placed a few additional stones on a grave. In time, some of the mounds became quite large.[9]

Looting Graves

Stories of valuable treasures being buried with Osages or just plain irreverent curiosity has caused many violations of the dead. One wonders how such people would react if someone did this to their grandmother's grave. It is true that some small tokens were intered with a dead Osage. More valuable tokens are commonly buried with white people, however. Think of all the gold wedding bands, gold and silver teeth, and cufflinks that lie in the white man's cemeteries. Why loot an Osage grave when such treasure offers greater profit to ghouls? To the morbid curious, the story about the top on an Indian skull being red is an absolute absurdity, so do not dig up an Osage grave to find out.

[9]David I. Bushnell, Jr., "Burials of the Algonquain, Siouan and Caddoan Tribes West of the Mississippi," *Smithsonian Institution, BAE, Bulletin 83,* (Government Printing Office: Washington, 1927), pp. 55-60.

Bibliography

Bushnell, David I., Jr., "Burials of the Algonquian, Siouan and Caddoan Tribes West of the Mississippi," *Smithsonian Institution, Bureau of American Ethnology, Bulletin 83,* Government Printing Office: Washington, 1927.

Dorsey, George A., "The Osage Mourning-War Ceremony," *American Anthropologist,* ns, no. 3, 4:1902, Jul-Sep.

La Flesche, Francis, "The Osage Tribe: The Rite of Vigil," *Smithsonian Institution, Bureau of American Ethnology, Thirty-Ninth Annual Report,* Government Printing Office: Washington, 1925.

_____, Francis, "War Ceremony and Peace Ceremony of the Osage Indians," *Smithsonian Institution, Bureau of American Ethnology, Bulletin 101,* U.S. Government Printing Office: Washington, 1939.

CHAPTER VIII

General Customs

Dress

Clothing of the Osages in the early 1800's was not yet greatly affected by trade. The greatest influence was in robes, beads, and bodily ornaments. While the buffalo robe continued to be used in greater numbers than blankets until about 1840, after that time trade blankets were more common. Trade beads were eagerly sought and quickly replaced the old beads. Porcupine quills were, however, still used until about 1850. Earrings and bells were the most evident body ornaments. Both men and women wore earrings but the men wore most of the bells. These bells were about the size of a large marble and were of the sleigh bell type. They were sewn onto leg and ankle bands and worn when dancing although a young man trying to catch the eyes of the girls may also have worn them.

Other decorations were also introduced as items of costume. Medallions were presented to important members of the tribe. Many of these were somewhat larger than a silver dollar and may have the image of a President on them. Military tunics were very popular presentation gifts, originally. Later, as the army changed uniform styles, these surplus army tunics became trade items. Many Osage women wore these tunics as a part of their wedding costume.

Osage men normally wore only a breech cloth and moccasins in warm weather. As the weather grew cooler, they usually added a trouser sleeve to each leg and a slip-over, long-sleeved, dresslike garment. The latter came down to a mid point between knee and hip. Originally, the breech cloth was softly tanned skins or woven buffalo hair. As trade with the white man grew, a soft fabric, like "melton," came into almost universal use. Trousers were made in two sleeve-like pieces, one for each leg. They fitted into the crotch and came high up the outside thigh to the hips where they were tied to the breech cloth belt. These "trousers" were made of deerskin and were frequently fringed on the outside seam. The fringes commemorated the fluttering of the eagles wings as the people soared down from the sky. Sometimes the slip-over top, also deerskin, was fringed on the sleeve seams and across the yoke in back.

Ceremonial moccasins were one piece and seamed down the toes in a single seam. Everyday and dress moccasins were made in two pieces with a single top piece sewn to a sole. These Osage moccasins did not have the so-called moccasin toe that is sometimes found among other tribes. Moccasins worn for everyday and those used for travel were made of buffalo hide. These may be made with or without the hair still on the leather. Extra moccasins were carried by war parties which went far afield. Dress moccasins were often made of dehaired deer skin except for the sole. At times, the toe was adorned with clan or tribal designs in bead work or dyes. Osage moccasins normally had a cuff turned down over a tie string. This string and cuff ran from a front slit around the heel and back to the front.

Women wore short sleeved pull-overs similar to those worn by the men but coming down below the knees. A wide buffalo hair, finger woven belt was worn around the waist. The men wore a similar belt but it was usually narrower. In cold weather, the women also wore two piece "trousers" similar to those worn by men. Male costumes were more colorful and fanciful than those the women wore. When wearing a full robe, the women covered both shoulders and arms. Men customarily left the right shoulder and arm uncovered.[1]

Both men and women wore robes. Some of the robes were more like shawls or capes. They were short and were primarily used to keep the shoulders warm. A full robe was long enough to cover the body down to the calf of the legs. When fabric trade blankets became plentiful, they replaced the short panther skin

[1] John D. Hunter, *Manners and Customs of Several Indian Tribes,* (Ross and Haines, Inc.: Minneapolis, MN 1957), p. 344.

and full buffalo robes. Trade blankets came in one, two, and three stripe grades. A one stripe blanket cost one prime beaver pelt. Two stripe blankets cost two beaver skins and the superior three stripe blanket cost three beaver skins or the equivalent in other peltry. This was the "Hudson Bay" blanket and trade system in use, both in the United States and in Canada. Later blankets appeared in many vari-colored stripes and a variety of designs. Blankets are worn with the stripes vertical.

Sometimes, a wide black fabric with stripes along one side was sold by the yard. This was the same material as strouding, used for leg wraps, and on some occasions the wide material was also called strouding. Ribbons of many colors were also traded by the yard. Blankets made of this black fabric were often adorned with "ribbon work". Osage women have every reason to be proud of their ribbon work because it is the most beautiful of all Indian ribbon work. Fabric shirts with ribbons also became popular as did wrap around skirts. As more and more of the animals became scarce, the old dress styles began to disappear.

Courtesies

Several chroniclers have commented on the speaking and listening habits of the Osage. In formal discussions, a speaker is heard to the end of his speech without interruption. They were accustomed to listen in patience with not a sign of boredom. To do otherwise in the presence of strangers was especially rude and offensive. Moderators were never used at meeting since they were not necessary. This trait often misled early missionaries and treaty commissioners. These worthies mistook the courtesy of hearing them out for acceptance of the words they spoke.[2]

[2]*Ibid.*, p. 50.

Types of Communication

Oral Language

Osage language is not rich in connectives or gender. In general, phrasing and often individual words are picture scenes. That is, they create mental pictures of what the speaker is trying to convey. To form the picture one must understand the culture. An example is wa ti an ka which is commonly interpreted as saucy. Yet, it refers to the actions of a calf cavorting in front of its mother. Playful would be a more accurate interpretation, but a calf performing such actions does have an air of sauciness. Another problem arises because many words derive their meanings from the circumstances in which they are used. This is not a matter of spoken context, but rather a matter of the environment where the word is used. Such a word is shin ka which means little, but when it is used in ceremonies it is often used to mean young. To aid in communication other means were used.

Body Language

The Osages were by constant daily practice excellent actors. They could watch a white man for a few minutes and perfectly mimic his every move and expression. In their speech with each other they had a system of symbolic body language and expressions that greatly enhanced the vocal language. When speaking as an orator, the men sought to impress the listeners. Treaty commissioners rarely understood the Osage language but they usually had a good idea of what was said before the interpreter spoke.[3]

---

[3]W.J. McGee, "The Siouan Indians," *Smithsonian Institution, BAE, 15th Annual Report,* (Government Printing Office: Washington, 1897), pp. 169-170.

Finger Talk

This body language was also employed when using finger talk. Pa se to pa lost his hearing when he was nine years old. He conversed in finger talk, sign language, from that time on. An American teacher of deaf and dumb students once visited with Pa se to pa in the deaf and dumb finger talk; they understood each other perfectly.[4] The various tribes could communicate in this manner without difficulty. Another communication means was really an extension of body language.

Dancing and Dramaturgy

Dancing and dramatization of ceremonies were frequently more expressive than words. In a few ways the ceremonial dramas resemble the ancient stylized Chinese theater. Both costumes and movements were symbols which expressed whole groups of ideas. In dancing, the direction of a turn and the speed of the step both conveyed meaning. A final means of communication were the graphic arts.

Pictorial Art

Unfortunately, some of the best Osage art symbols were rendered in perishable media. For example, it was drawn in the soil or it was painted on the body. Archaeologist sometimes conclude that the Osages had a limited amount of graphic art. If one based their thinking on the pottery shards found at Osage village sites, this conclusion would be accurate. The Osages left few if any signs of an extensive development of graphic arts on permanent materials. Their pottery was unadorned utilitarian vessels. Baskets had some designs woven into them, but almost

[4]J.G. Sanders, *Who's Who Among Oklahoma Indians,* (Trave Company: Oklahoma City, 1927), p. 170.

all of these have perished. Their clothing which was often ornate was cast away for fabric clothing and with them went many designs.

We do have some designs that were worked into fabric clothing. Ribbon work was appliqued to the clothing in color but the colors were in good taste and did not clash. Most of the ribbon work designs were adapted from parfleche designs. It is through ribbon work that one sees most of the Osage graphic art today. Some Osage beadwork still exists and this work also preserves some of the Osage designs. It must be noted that almost all of this beadwork is done with trade beads and not the native beads. We have never seen an example of Osage quill work, although some undoubtedly still exists. Examples of dyed designs on articles made of skins still exist in sizable numbers.

Sacred Osage colors were red, blue, yellow, and dark which is more commonly interpreted as black. White is often used in beadwork and ribbon work. Another favored color is magenta or a purple-red which is especially becoming to a dark complexion. Although the symbolism of the various colors are somewhat variable, we will risk censure and list some of the symbolism.

White, symbolizes the peaceful day which, in turn, represents a long life.

Blue, also symbolizes a clear sky or peaceful day.

Red, represented the rising sun which is a symbol of life in all forms.

Yellow, represented the beneficial rays of the sun which sustains life in all forms. It also represented sham or bluff.

Black, represented death, the unrelenting destruction of fire, the peaceful benefits of fire, and the west or unknown darkness from which all life comes and to which all life returns.

Tints and shades, such as pink and magenta, of these colors represented either the same thing or degrees of intensity. Green was also used in ribbon work, but we are not aware of its symbolism. We would risk the guess that it symbolizes the evergreen cedar which was a symbol of old age.

Osage graphic art is geometric, that is, it tends to be angular rather than curvy and leans toward stylized forms which represents the true figure. For example, diamonds represent a layered thing such as the upper worlds. Thus, a series of four diamonds represents the four upper worlds. However, the diamond is also used to symbolize the turtle. A single diamond standing alone sometimes represents the mouth of a symbolic head. All life passes through the mouth of the symbolic head before it can possess a body. In a diamond within a diamond, the outer diamond represents the mouth and the inner diamond represents the tongue. This is a symbol of life returning to the mouth and traveling down the tongue which represents the spirit path.

While most of the Osage designs are geometric some do have the wavy lines of the eastern woodland tribes. Possibly these are very old designs developed when the Osages still lived in the eastern woodlands. The geometric designs probably developed as they moved to the Great Plains.

We have placed a Ho e ka on the front cover for good reason. Red is the color of life and the Ho e ka is a trap which ensnares all life. The four winds are the breath of life. Thus, the Ho e ka represents life on earth and that is the subject of our book. This symbol, the Ho e ka, is used by most of the Siouan peoples.

A Ho e ka is frequently shown as a rectangle with a missing short side. Sometimes it shows one, two, or three winds but more commonly all four winds. The symbolism of the one or two winds comes from the mythology. At first the winds blew in only one direction at a time, either north or south. It would blow to the south, then turn and blow back to the north. Three winds north, east, and west were good winds but the south wind brought sickness and death to the people and killed the plants. For these reasons the south wind was sometimes omitted.

Zigzag lines often meant the seven bends in the river of life or if only four are shown it meant the four valleys of life's journey. The latter referred to the four stages of life. These were childhood, young adult, mature adult, and old age. We have never had a good

157

understanding of the symbolism in the seven bends of the river of life. It has been said, that one has seven crises in their lifetime. Possibly, the bends of the river represents these turning points of life.

The following stylized symbols are Osage and appear on ornaments, paintings, fabric work, beadwork, and dyed rawhide. They represent enough of Osage graphic art to create a question of validity to the belief that the Osages were very limited in graphic art. Enough has survived to indicate the Osages communicated with a rich heritage of graphic art.

Explanation of the Designs

Fig. 12 is seven variations of the Ho e ka. The first is a full design, as shown on our cover. It represents the snare and all four winds. In the second variation, the south wind has been omitted. Only the north and south winds are shown in the third design. The single wind that blew both north and south is shown in the fifth variation. Only the snare is shown in the fourth design. In the sixth and seventh design, the east and west winds are shown on the sides of the snare.

Fig. 13 shows six variations of the diamond theme. To the left of the center the three diamond variations represents the symbolic mouth. In the two with diamonds within a diamond the inner diamond represents a tongue. The center series of four diamonds and the series of four in the upper right represent the four upper worlds. In the lower right is another representation of the four upper worlds. It may well be that all of these diamond symbols were originally derived from the turtle.

Fig. 14 is a conventional representation of the morning star. This design was originally cut from a white mussel shell and worn as a gorget. Silver and German silver morning star designs became common after trade with the white man started. In time, the design was worn as a gorget as well as a neckerchief slide.

158

Fig. 12. Ho e ka Variations

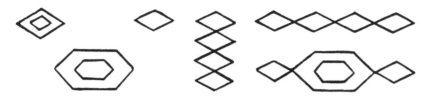

Fig. 13. Diamond Variations

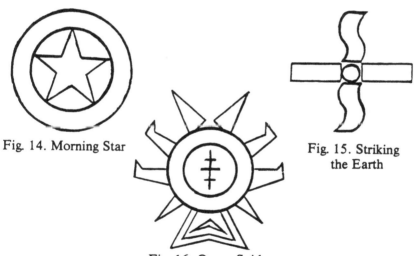

Fig. 14. Morning Star

Fig. 15. Striking
the Earth

Fig. 16. Osage Spider

159

Fig. 17 Design from a Large Parfleche
(Courtesy of the Osage Tribal Museum.)

160

Fig. 18. Design from a Small Parfleche
(Courtesy of the Osage Tribal Museum.)

161

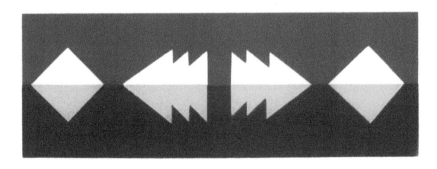

Fig. 19. Ribbonwork Designs
(Courtesy of the Osage Tribal Museum.)

162

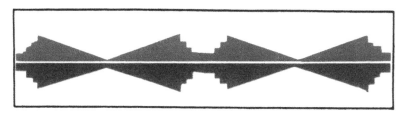

Fig. 20. Ribbonwork Design
(Courtesy of Bessie Tinker.)

Fig. 21. Beadwork Rosette from a Moccasin
(Courtesy of the Osage Tribal Museum.)

Fig. 22. Beadwork Design from a Moccasin
(Courtesy of the Osage Tribal Museum.)

163

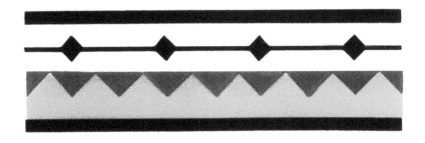

Fig. 23. Beadwork Head Band from an Osage Bonnet
(Southwest Museum, Los Angeles, CA.)

Fig. 24. Design from a Beaded Vest
(Courtesy of the Osage Tribal Museum.)

Fig. 25. Beaded Design from a Girl's Moccasin
(Courtesy of the Osage Tribal Museum.)

Fig. 26. Beaded Design of the
Morning Star
*(Courtesy of the Osage
Tribal Museum.)*

Fig. 27. Beaded Design of the
Evening Star
*(Courtesy of the Osage
Tribal Museum.)*

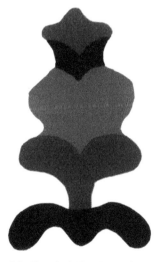

Fig. 29. Beaded Design of the
Four Upper Worlds
Resting on the Red
Oak
*(Courtesy of the Osage
Tribal Museum.)*

Fig. 28. Beaded Design of the
"Tree of Life"
*(Courtesy of the Osage
Tribal Museum.)*

165

Fig. 15 is a design drawn from the ceremony of Striking the Earth. The center circle represents the midday sun. On the left and right of the "sun" are two straight lines which represent the sun's path. Two wavy vertical lines represent the beneficial rays of the sun. In a broad sense, this design represented the unity of the Osage people with themselves and with nature.

Fig. 16 is a stylized design of a spider. Some say it represented the crawfish that gave the people the four sacred colors of dark, blue, red, and yellow. It seems more likely to represent the black widow spider. Osage mythology relates, the spider's web like the Ho e ka is a snare which traps all living things and holds them here on earth until they die.

Fig. 17 is a design from a large parfleche. Each of the two flaps of the parfleche had the same design. No Osage woman needed to place her name on her parfleche to identify them as hers. Her design was her signature and identified the parfleche without question.

Fig. 18 is a design from a small parfleche. This was a small single flap parfleche. The Osage and other Siouan peoples almost always outlined their parfleche designs in dark, meaning a dark color.

Fig. 19 illustrates three ribbonwork designs. The variety and amount of ribbonwork far exceeds any other source of Osage designs. Fig. 20 is a final ribbonwork design which is currently a popular pattern. Most of these designs trace their origins to the old parfleche designs.

Fig. 21 is a beadwork rosette. This particular design and Fig. 22 were combined on a pair of man's dress moccasins. The rosette was over the toe and the straight design met in a "vee" in front of the rosette.

Fig. 23 is a beadwork design from the head band of a bonnet. It would be interesting to know the story behind this design.

Fig. 24 is from a beaded vest. As a general rule, a cross in Osage designs represents the four winds. This design and the other vest designs were laid on a black background.

Fig. 25 is a design from a girl's moccasin. It ran up the leg in a vertical position with the central theme alternating in direction. The three tined figures may be a variation of the Ho e ka. Certainly the central theme suggests a stylization of thunder. This would be an interesting design to "read".

Fig. 26 is another version of the morning star. The ten points and ten valleys of the inner star are especially interesting as is the absence of the outer circle. Depicting this in black and red is a beautiful concept, since the morning star represents the passing of night and the coming of day.

Fig. 27 is a design representing the evening star. The color choice of blue and red is significant. If one looks at the evening star it has a red color when cast against the blue vault of the coming night. This star symbolizes the passing of day and coming of night.

Fig. 28 is a design of the tree of life. This was the cedar tree with its red wood and green fronds. The trunk has shaggy yellow bark which is symbolic of old age. Cedar is the symbol of a long life.

Fig. 29 is a design depicting the four upper worlds resting on the red oak tree. The tree stands in the dark undisturbed waters of the earth. Like the cedar the red oak was a symbol of life, but it symbolized many descendants, rather than a long life.

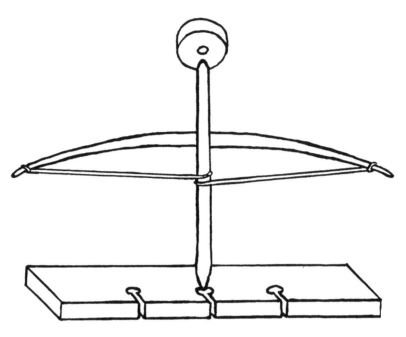

Fig. 30. Friction Fire Starting Components

Fire Building

When building a fire, especially ceremonial fires, the tinder was ignited by the friction method. One of two well dried sticks had holes drilled through the center and slits cut from one edge to the holes. The slits allowed air to enter the hole. A second stick was rounded at the working end and twirled back and forth rapidly between the palms. This generated friction in the wood hole and the wood ignited. By gentle blowing into the slit as tinder is added to the glowing ember in the hole, a flame is coaxed into the tinder which is then placed into the laid fire wood.[5]

---

[5] Francis La Flesche, "The Osage Tribe: The Rite of Vigil," *Smithsonian Institution, BAE, 39th Annual Report,* (Government Printing Office: Washington, 1925), p. 224.

A variation of this method was used to ignite ordinary fires. (See Fig. 30.) A hand piece with an indentation which fit on the top of the twirling stick was added. Suet or tallow was used to lubricate the top piece. A bowed stick had a leather thong attached to it at one end. The thong was passed around the twirling stick once and then held at the other end of the arched stick. By holding the bow and string in the right hand and the hand piece in the left hand a push and pull motion of the bow would spin the twirling stick and generate friction.

A similar device was used to bore holes and to cut beads from mussel shells. Broken flint projectile points were reworked, leaving the shaft end intact but the body was worked into an awl like shaft. These were attached to what would be the friction end of the twirling stick in fire making. Some small reworked projectile heads had a forked working end rather than an awl end. By cutting a shell half way through from both sides a rough bead complete with the hole was obtained. We have a few awl drills in our collection, but the beads, bead drills, and mussel shells with the holes were given away in the innocence of youth. Evidently, the beads were smoothed after cutting for they were smooth and symmetrical. They were about the size of a large pea. All of these beads were white as were all the mussel shells with bead cut-out holes. Yet, we have found quite a number of blue mussel shells and a few rare pink shells in the same locality.

Fire making with flint to flint and steel to flint was also practiced by the Osages. However, in our own experience we have found both friction methods to be easier and faster than flint. Possibly with greater experience, making fire with flint would prove more satisfactory. Starting a fire from scratch, however, was often avoided by the Osages. The two "houses in the middle" customarily kept a fire going at all times. Anyone could take embers from these fires to start their own fire. In fact, it was considered beneficial to have a fire started by embers from the chief's fire.

Hair Customs

We thought young Osage men and women would like to know how their ancestors let each other know when they wanted to marry. The man showed his interest by strutting around the village in all his finery. As today, the women were more subtle. When a woman was ready to marry, she wore her long hair in front of her shoulders. Married women always wore their hair behind the shoulders.

Respect Toward Relatives

In ancient times a newly married couple lived with the bride's parents. However, there is some evidence that this changed and the couple lived with the groom's parents. With exposure to European culture, the practice of establishing a new domicile grew in importance. In any event, the in-law was always treated with the utmost respect. All male descendants of the mother's brothers were also regarded with the highest esteem and joking was never practiced between the child and their male maternal cousins. These customs had all but disappeared by the 1930's. The maternal uncle and his male descendants had lost their importance in tribal life. While the maternal uncle was greatly respected he no longer had a say in family affairs. His sons were treated as any cousin would be treated in the majority culture.[6]

Parfleches

Parfleches were so widely used by the Osages that they and their uses must be included in Osage customs. The word parfleche is a compound of two French words, par, to enter and fleche a projectile such as an arrow. In its compound form it refers to

[6]Betty R. Nett, "Osage Kinship System," *Southwestern Journal of Anthropology,* 8:180-181, 1952.

something that would deflect missiles. Originally the term was applied to rawhide shields, but in time it came to be applied to articles made of rawhide. Eventually, the term came to mean the rawhide storage bags. Customarily parfleches were made in pairs, since two could be made from one buffalo hide. They were always made of rawhide, never tanned leather. The hair side was invariably to the inside but the hair was almost totally removed. Because the making of parfleches reveals so much about Osage life, we will give a detailed account of how they were made.

Making a parfleche starts with stretching the hide. This is a hard and tricky task since the green hide is heavy and must be carefully stretched. Stretching is accomplished by slitting a series of holes in the hide on its perimeter. The slits are then slipped over stakes driven in the ground. If the tension is too tight the slits will tear out; if it is too light the hide will be wavy and the hump will make a bad place.

When the hide has dried, it is fleshed and scraped while it is still in the stakes. It is desirable to make the flesh side as white as possible. To lighten the color, the flesh side is repeatedly scrubbed with water. Yucca or "soapweed" juice was sometimes used as a detergent. Dried bulrush, sandstone, and sometimes dried buffalo tongue was used to scrub with. After several scrubbings and flushings the hide was a very light cream color and was odor free.

The next step depended on the practice of the individual making the parfleche. Some preferred to apply the design directly on the untreated hide while others would put one or two coats of waterproofing on before applying the design. Usually, a partially coated hide is reflected in a design with sharp clear lines. Untreated hides often have blurred lines. These coatings were usually hide-hoof-horn glue-like but thin mixtures. Prickly pear cactus juice was also used as well as thinned cedar gum. When one or two coats had been applied, the hide was ready for the design.

The design may come from the tribal myths, from the division and clan, or they may be a creation of the maker. Osage women would sometimes look directly at the sun and then squeeze their eyes shut tightly. This resulted in a visual display of colors and geometric shapes. From these, they would create designs. (See Figs. 17-18.) It is interesting that parfleches were made in pairs, one from each side of the hide. As a matter of further interest, each of the two flaps of a parfleche was adorned with the same design. While this is suggestive of the two grand divisions and four ceremonial pauses, no record was found that would confirm the suggestion.

Colors used were both mineral and vegetable. In use, the colors were mixed with water and cactus juice or cedar gum. This was molded into a disk shaped cake and allowed to dry. The color was applied to a wet hide. Osages customarily outlined their designs in "dark", which meant any dark color. On parfleches this was often a blackish brown, but it may be any dark shade. Two coats of wax finish was then put on the design. This was done by splitting a beaver's tail and heating it. By rubbing the cut side of the tail over the design it became waxed with beaver tail wax. After this treatment, the hide was carefully dried.

When the hide was dry, the flesh side was placed on a pad of grass. A rounded stream stone was held in the right hand and the hide was struck with glancing blows. Each blow would remove a patch of hair. At the same time it made the rawhide more pliable and tended to implant the design into the hide. Other methods of dehairing were also used, but the result was not as satisfactory as hammering.

The dehaired, adorned, waterproofed rawhide was now ready to be cut-out and shaped into a parfleche. A flint knife which was well sharpened was used in ancient times, in modern times, a very sharp steel knife was used. Dry rawhide is very hard to cut, so a sharp knife was essential. Wet rawhide is much easier to cut than dry hide but it has the feel of wet rubber, so it too, requires a sharp knife. The parfleche was made in one piece without any seams or divided compartments. In essence, it consisted of two side flaps and two end flaps with a bottom. First the side flaps were folded upward and then the adorned end flaps were folded over the turned-up sides.

The lashing holes were usually burned through the rawhide. Cut holes tended to tear or elongate. Burning hardened the rawhide around the hole and was more lasting. Osages put a single hole at the ends of the flap and a set of two holes in the center edge. When laced closed, the parfleche was almost completely waterproof.

Bibliography

Hunter, John D., *Manners and Customs of Several Indian Tribes,* Ross and Haines, Inc.: Minneapolis, MN, 1957, reprint of the original published in 1823.

McGee, W.J., "The Siouan Indians," *Smithsonian Institution, Bureau of American Ethnology, Fifteenth Annual Report,* Government Printing Office: Washington, 1897.

Nett, Betty R., "Osage Kinship System," *Southwestern Journal of Anthropology,* 8:1952.

Sanders, J.G., *Who's Who Among Oklahoma Indians,* Trave Company: Oklahoma City, 1927.

PART

II

MYTHS

CHAPTER IX

Genesis Myths

Introduction

Ne ke a, in a free translation, means Sayings of the Ancient Men. The name is used to describe the mythical stories of the origin of the clans. Osage personal names, ceremonially bestowed, are all Ne ke a names or names that refer to the mythical stories of the clan's origin. In almost all cases these personal names refer to events or a manifestation of Wa kon ta.

Osage myths were not centered around individuals as were the Greek, Roman, and Germanic myths. In some of the myths it may appear that an individual is named as the hero. However, it must be noted that these are names of clans and not individuals, although Osage expression make them seem to be names of individuals. The people act as a group in Osage mythology. In the myths of Western Civilization, the stress is on the individual's relationship with the Gods. In Osage myths, the emphasis is on the relationship of the people with the many manifestations of the Mysterious Being of the Universe. This concept of unity of many in the being of one is similar to the Holy Trinity in Christianity. That is, God the Father, God the Son, and God the Holy Spirit. One may illustrate the concept with a match book. If all twenty matches are lit at the same time, there is only one flame but twenty matches.

Most of the recorded Osage myths are about the selection of life symbols, commonly called totems. Life symbols were role models for living ones life. Full appreciation of the significance of these symbols is sometimes difficult. For example, the Little Rock of the Marsh is a life symbol. How could a human emulate a rock? When one considers the durability and peacefulness of stone, and the stoic acceptance of what comes its way, the keenness of Osage thoughts emerge. It is easy to stimulate the mind with heroic deeds; it is another matter to meditate on the nature of a mundane object made by the Great Creator.

As one reads Osage mythology another comparison with Western Civilization emerges. The Osages considered themselves to be a part of the world around them. In the myths of Western Civilization, man is constantly in conflict with his environment. To phrase it differently, the Osage myths are in harmony with nature while myths of Western Civilization are in conflict with nature. In Osage minds, man is a part of nature and must live with nature. Western minds may not think man is superior to nature, but Western man acts and writes as though he must change nature in order to live.

When choosing life symbols from creatures and objects of nature, the Osages considered the traits that would help them live out their lives. They were scholars of the natural world. However, they were also scholars of man and his actions. This is evident in the myths. The references to a "move to a new country," as well as many other incidents show the restless quest of the unknown. They understood this searching urge of mankind. Reactions when messengers return with news of strange new things also show a great comprehension of human traits.

We have tried to forewarn the reader so he or she will not adventure into Osage mythology with a mind-set of Western Civilization. Osage mythology is a new world were all is not as it seems to be. It is a world where our mental gears must be shifted to a new unused position. The world that could have helped us comprehend, no longer exists. When the buffalo perished, the hoop of the Osage world was broken.

Different Versions

While the versions of the different clans agree in general outline they differ in some details. To a great extent this is due to a special emphasis placed on the role of a particular clan. For this reason, wherever possible, we have given more than one version and clan identification. In most cases, the added details add interesting sidelights to the basic story.

Like most oral myths, the Osage myths have many repetitions to aid the memory. We have paraphrased the original form to eliminate the repetitions. This has caused a loss of tempo and expression. Since the translation also loses the beauty of the Osage language, our versions are even more flawed. Oral myths, when reduced to the written words cannot present the flickering firelight, the odors of the House of Mysteries, or the dramaturgy that was present when these myths were recited. Thus, our versions written here are pale shadows of the true myths.

Genesis Myth

(Panther Clan Version)

After the people acquired souls in the first upper world, the Hun ka began to talk with each other. They talked about going below to the earth. Finally, they decided to ask the four great Gods for help.[1] First, they appealed to the God of Day, the sun. Grandfather told them they were no persons, but he would always be with them.[2] Now they spoke to the Goddess of Night, the moon. Grandmother promised them her perpetual assistance and promised them they would live together as a people. Next, they prayed to the Male Star, morning star. He promised them aid and his constant presence, but he also promised them calm and peaceful days. At last, they spoke to the Female Star, evening star. She told them they would see the four great divisions of the days.[3] With these assurances, the Little Ones decided to descend

[1] These Gods were all manifestations of Wa kon ta, the Creator of the Universe.

[2] No person meant they had no bodies, and therefore, they were spirits. This is to say, that as spirits they could not live on earth.

[3] This is a reference to the four divisions in a person's life; childhood, young adult, mature adult, and old age.

179

to earth.

Realizing that none of them knew the way, they asked Hun ka Ah hu tun to search out a way.[4] He led the people downward through the four heavens. Four times he soared in wide circles and then without pause he dived downward through the standing clouds.[5] He came in sight of the tops of seven trees, where he waited.[6] The people alit in the tops of the trees and firmly gripped the branches with their feet. All the earth below the branches was covered with water. The people became desperate and they begged Hun ka Wa tse ka wa to help them.[7] He went to seek help from spider-like, water spider; black bean-like, water beetle; and whitleather-like, white leech; who offered to seek help, but furnished no solution.

At last, Radiant Star came to Opon Tun ka, the Big Elk.[8] To help the Little Ones, he threw himself violently on the earth. Huge waves radiated away from the impact. Again he threw himself with greater force upon the waters and they began to ebb. A third time the mighty elk threw himself to the earth and again the waters were lowered. For the fourth time the noble elk threw himself down and the soil of the earth appeared, to become dry and habitable.

Big Elk then called for the four winds, the breath of Wa kon ta, to come dry the land. He called first the wind of the rising run, then

[4] Hun ka ah hu tun or Hun ka Having Wings is a sub-clan of the Hu lah, Eagle, clan.

[5] Standing clouds was the Osage term for cumulous clouds which sometimes became thunder clouds. The term specifically applies to the fluffy cumulous clouds, however.

[6] There were seven clans in the Hun ka sub-division.

[7] Watsa ka wa or Radiant Star is the star name for the Owners of the Black Bear clan. This is the clan's correct earth name, but it is usually called the Black Bear clan. It is closely related to the Panther clan.

[8] The elk was never absent from a place of great events.

he called loudly over the lands of the earth for the cedar wind.[9] He called for the wind from sundown and warm winds of the south.[10] Once the winds were gathered, the Elk endowed them with the breath of life and commanded them to blow over the earth.

For a final time the huge elk threw himself to the ground. He rolled on the earth and left scattered hairs from his body clinging to the soil of the earth. His hairs became grasses and other plants. Useful animals would feed on the grasses and other plants furnished the Little Ones with food wherever they wandered. The elk then made the ridges of his spine and rounded hills of his rump. Gaps in the ridges were made from his curved neck and the bluffs were made from his nose tip. His horns became the streams with their groves of trees. Now the elk gave the people his last gift, "Take my forehead, for I have made it a snare for all life, none can escape from it."

With the help of the elk the Hun ka could now walk over the land. They traveled over the earth until they came to a prairie devoid of trees. At this place, they came upon a crawfish. The people recoiled in fear at the sight of this dangerous person. Their leader moistened his right index finger to point at this fearsome creature.[11] Quickly, the creature identified himself as Hun Ka Moh en ka Shin ka or Little Earth. Four times Little Earth went deep into the ground. First, he brought up dark soil, black, next he brought blue soil to the surface. After he had brought red and yellow mud to the surface he spoke to the people, "These are to be your sacred colors, you must use them to paint your bodies." When he had finished instructing them in the use of the colors, he cautioned them to remove the colors before the last rays of the sun were gone.

[9]The winds resided among the cedar trees, but the north wind was especially the wind from the cedars.

[10]The south wind had a bad reputation among the Osages. While the warmth was appreciated, the hot south winds of August often brought sickness and death.

[11]Because the people lacked weapons when they first came to earth, Wa kon ta gave them the power to kill with the moist finger.

"We have nothing from which to make our bodies," cried the people.[12] Now they came upon the great Red Boulder, the mighty Black Boulder, the White Boulder, and the Yellow Boulder. All of these promised to help. The boulders noted that they were difficult to overcome by death and all who struck them stumbled and fell. Those who set teeth in them suffered pain. Because they were firm, evil forces turned aside to avoid the boulders. The people continued their search and came to the Soft Yellow Rock and the Friable Rock. These promised to aid the Little Ones in sickness.[13] Still the people searched until they came to the Little Rock of the Marsh. Now the Little Rock spoke to the people, "Observe my locks, moss, that floats around the edges of my head." He reminded them that they would see the four divisions of days. Their hair would grow thin with age like his.[14]

Radiant Star was sent out to find plants that could be used for food. He went to a marsh and brought back the tubers of the great bur-reed. These were deemed all right for emergency use but too hard to gather in large quantities. Next he brought back the tuber of the water lily with notched leaf. While these were good food they too were rejected. Black Bear next brought the water lily,

[12]This expression refers to a role model for the shaping of character. At this point in the myth they were seeking symbols.

[13]A remedy for illness was a steam vapor bath. These two kinds of stones were heated and had water poured on them, thus, generating steam.

[14]The Black Bear clan commemorated this event by cutting their children's hair bare on the top and with a fringe around the edges. The Little Rock of the Marsh is a peace symbol for this clan. Note should also be taken of the numbers four and seven. Thirteen is another number frequently mentioned. The symbolism of these numbers is not always clear. However, the original tribal organization consisted of four divisions and the Hun ka consisted of seven clans to make one of these four divisions. The seven Dakota fireplaces or clans may have been the parent Siouan stock. Yet, the Osages could have been the parent Siouan stock. It seems splinters would seek new country and go farther from the homeland while the parent stock would remain nearer the homeland. In recorded history, the discontent have migrated; the contented have remained in place.

American lotus, with yellow flowers and large bowl shaped leaves. This was declared an excellent food plant. Still Radiant Star went again to the marsh. This time he brought back duck potatoes from the arrowhead plant. These too were accepted as good food. Next he went along a stream bank and brought back the walnut sized tubers of the groundnut. The elder brothers declared these to be suitable food. For the last time Black Bear went to the stream bank where there was a grove of trees. Here he found a vine with small white and violet flowers. He gathered pods from above and below ground. The elders boiled these and declared them good when boiled.[15]

Genesis Myth

(Black Bear Version)

It has been said in this house, the Little Ones were to become a people. The idea threw the people into deep thought. They sat in great perplexity, for they had hoped to make the first of the upper worlds their home. It was too late for this now, they had made their first downward soaring. They gave some thought to making the second of the upper worlds their home, but already the people were again downward soaring. The third and fourth upper worlds were also passed in their soarings.

As they soared over the earth they found it covered with undisturbed water. Finally they alit on the tops of seven great rocks. The seventh rock was black and it spoke to them, offering itself as a life symbol; the red rock also offered itself as a life symbol. Everyone knew that they could not live atop the water like the water beetle; the water spider; the water strider; and the red breasted leech. All of these tried to help the Little Ones, but all they could do was to offer themselves as life symbols.

[15] Francis La Flesche, "The Osage Tribe: Rite of the Chiefs; Sayings of the Ancient Men," *Smithsonian Institution, BAE, 36th Annual Report,* (Government Printing Office: Washington, 1921), pp. 157-185.

183

Then the people spoke to the Big Elk. They said, "It is not possible for the Little Ones to live on the surface of the water, O, grandfather, nor can we cause the water to become dry land. We ask you to help us solve this dilemma." The Big Elk then threw himself upon the water and brought up the dark soil. Again he threw himself upon the water and brought up the blue soil of the earth. For a third time the elk plunged into the water and brought up the red soil. A final time he threw himself upon the waters and brought the yellow soil to the surface. Then the elk spoke to the people, "I who stand before you, am Hun ka, a sacred person, the Big Elk by name. I am Maker of the Earth's Soil and Maker of the Land, these shall be personal names among you."

The people asked the one who had made his body of the panther, to go forth to explore the land. He returned stumbling and tripping again and again in his haste. The news he brought was of a strange fear-inspiring person. Now the leaders thrust their index fingers in their mouths to moisten them and give to them the killing power. Speaking to them, the strange person said, "I am a Hun ka, a sacred person," the people marveled that he spoke their language. Continuing to speak to the Little Ones, the stranger said, "I am a Hun ka who has come from the midst of the stars. Little Chief, Star Chief, Radiant Star, and Star That Travels are my names." With this, the people agreed to banish all anger and hatred toward the stranger. Then they agreed that henceforth the stranger's names would become personal names among them. Because he was sacred and spoke their language fluently, they also adopted the personal names of Sacred Stranger and Speaks Fluently, in his honor.

Now the one with a panther's body was sent to find materials for sacred objects. He soon returned to report he had found a strange creature. They came to the place where the strange animal dwelt. An elder brother thrust his index finger in his mouth, quickly he withdrew it and pointed his finger at the animal. The bird fell in death with its feathers scattered on the ground. Quickly, the people gathered around the fallen swan, its unusual features excited their interest. Its feet and bill were black and became the symbol of war. Since its feathers were white they made White Swan, White Bird, and White Feather personal names in honor of this white bird. From the curve of its neck they made their war standard.

Again the people asked the one with a panther body to seek material for ceremonial objects. He brought back a rock fragment which was made a life symbol but was not suitable for a sacred object. The same was true of the rock that explodes with heat, shale; the white rock, limestone; and the yellow rock, sandstone.

A fifth time panther body went forth, he returned gasping for breath as he gave his news. He had found an animal of some kind. It was formidable in appearance and had cloven feet. The sharp horns on its head curved inward. Now the Little Ones approached the animal making the four ceremonial pauses. As the people viewed the female buffalo, they described the ceremonial uses of the animal.[16] From the skin they made the ceremonial robes. Thus, they also created a personal name, The Sacred Robe. Other personal names coming from the buffalo were Woman of the Spine, Buffalo Horn, and Maker of the Head.

The Little Ones needed a knife, so they again sent the one with a panther body out to look for suitable material. He returned with the stone that flakes, quartz, but it was not suitable. After a second journey he returned with a piece of hard flint, quartzite, this was also rejected. The third time he returned with the red, round-handled knife. This was accepted and became the ceremonial knife of the Little Ones. To commemorate the consecration of this knife, the people took the personal names of Red Knife and Sacred Knife.[17]

Genesis Myth

(Elder Tsi shu Version)

The Tsi shu spoke to each other, it did not seem impossible to

[16] The Osages preferred the young cow buffalo for both meat and robes.

[17] La Flesche, *36th Ann. Rpt., op. cit.,* pp. 219-237.

live down below. They spoke to the messenger and asked him to search for a way they could go below. He hastened on his way and found the bird that had no evil.[18] With the aid of the bird that had no evil, they soared downward. They came to the earth in four soarings and landed in the tops of seven trees.

Then they stood on the land and moved onward over the earth. After passing through a valley they came to a cliff of white rock. Here, they made White Rock a personal name. At last, they realized they could not journey in this unorganized fashion. So they sent the messenger to search for a way.

Younger Brother, the messenger, went forth five times and brought back a different colored flint each time. He brought back red, blue, yellow-streaked, black, and white flint but each kind was rejected as unsuitable. On the sixth journey younger brother found the round-handled knife which was accepted as the ceremonial knife.

Again, Younger Brother was sent to find material for a ceremonial club. He brought back the smooth bark hickory; the red oak, and the dark-wood tree, red bud; but none of these were suitable. On his fourth trip, he brought back the willow which was accepted as the proper material for the ceremonial club.

They took the round-handled knife from its honored resting place. As they did this they noticed the knife was awe-inspiring and mysterious. So they decided to make Mysterious Knife a personal name. Now they lifted the knife and cut four strips from the willow, one for each of the four directions. When they finished carving, the long club was shaped like the back of a fish.[19]

Wishing to test the merits of the ceremonial club, the Elder Brothers, again, sent the messenger to explore the land. He returned with the news that he had found the footprints of a person

[18]This bird without evil refers to the immature golden eagle also called mottled eagle. The expression came from observing that the other birds did not dislike this eagle.

[19]In this description, the myth is saying the club had projections like the dorsal fins of a fish.

with cloven feet. Again he went forth and returned with the information that he had seen the strange person. When asked what the stranger was like in appearance and disposition, the messenger described his formidable appearance, and the weapons he carried.

They took the ceremonial club from its resting place and sought the strange person. The people traveled in single file and made four pauses as they approached the strange creature. When all was ready Elder Brother raised the club and waved it, our grandfather lunged forward as from a sudden shock.[20] Again the club was quickly brandished in the air. Our grandfather staggered. Now for the third time Elder Brother flailed the air with the club and grandfather dropped to his knees, stunned by the shock. A fourth time the club rose and our grandfather fell dead to the ground.

The people hastened to cut the skin of the left hind leg. They tasted the fat which was sweet and pleasant to the taste. A thin strip was cut from the skin of the left leg, the people noticed it did not stretch, so it was useful. It was such a strap that made Strong Strap a personal name. Strap Maker and Slender Strap were also made personal names. From the center of the skin they made a shield. The horns also became a source of personal names such as Curved Horns and Outspread Horns.[21]

Genesis Myth

(Wearers of Symbolic Locks Version, Tsi shu)[22]

The people whose abode was in the heavens, assembled so

[20] Elder Brother refers to the Elder Tsi shu clan. Our grandfather was a term of respect for the buffalo.

[21] La Flesche, *36th Ann. Rpt., op. cit.,* pp. 254-269.

[22] This paraphrase was made by Dr. Francis La Flesche. However, since some editorial changes were made, the paraphrase was not placed in quotes.

they might meditate upon the means by which they would descend to earth and come into bodily existence. They decided that the eagle was the only person who could safely conduct them to the earth. They, therefore, appealed to him and he led them downward. The people, led by the eagle, came to the earth and alighted upon seven trees: The full-grown shagbark hickory; The young shagbark; The red oak; The thick barked bitter hickory; The smooth-barked bitter hickory; and The willow.[23]

The people found that in the willow tree there was a mystical power – a power for resisting the forces that sought to harm life. They wished to cut the tree to make a part of its body a Wa ho pe, a sacred object for ceremonial use. They sent their Sho ka or official messenger, to find the material out of which to make a knife. Four times he went out to make search, but without success. At the fifth time he brought home a knife which he had made from a grayish stone. He had made for it a handle that was round. The people accepted the knife, consecrated it for ceremonial use and called it the round-handled knife. With this sacred knife they cut from the body of the tree four small pieces, which they threw into the air as sacred offerings, one to each of the four winds. Blood flowed from each of the four wounds made with the ceremonial knife.

Then the people, using their sacred knife, proceeded to cut down the tree, to shave the trunk to a proper size, and to shape it for a club. This club they called Wa ho pe, sacred, and consecrated it for ceremonial use. The natural color of the wood did not satisfy the people and they regarded the sacred article as incomplete. Then, as though by a common understanding and consent, they hastened to gather leaves and dry twigs. These they placed in a great pile, to which they set fire, and the smoke and flames tinged the darkened heavens with a reddish hue – a color pleasing and satisfying to the minds of the people. It resembled

[23]Dr. La Flesche notes that Pa le wa we ha ta mentioned seven trees but gave the names of only six. We believe the seventh tree was the Ba po or alder tree. The alder was a life symbol of the Tsi shu Peacemaker clan, their myths say they landed in this tree.

the color cast upon the eastern sky as the sun rises and which the people always hailed with joy and uplifted hands. It was this color they put on the symbolic club to add to it the life-giving power of the sun.

The weapon was thus finished, and there remained nothing more to do with it but to test its magical power. For this purpose the people sent their official messenger to a far-off country to search for some creature upon which to make the test. The messenger returned in the evening of the day, weary and footsore, to report that he had been to a valley where he saw nothing worthy of notice. Again he went out and returned from a second valley to report that he had found nothing. He was bidden to go again, and in the evening of that day he came home to report that he had been to a third valley, where he had seen the footprints of a person.[24] The footprints showed the person's feet to be cloven, and the grasses upon which he had trodden were crushed. To commemorate this event, the people agreed to name their children, Crushed With His Feet. For the fourth time the messenger was sent out, and in the evening of the day he came home to report that he had been to a fourth valley, where he saw the person of the footprints, whom he described as a person of formidable appearance and bearing upon his head curved horns. To make this report memorable, the people agreed to name their children Curved Horns. The messenger gave a graphic description of the face of the person, and from this the people agreed to name their children Buffalo Bull Face.

Upon hearing the last report, the keeper of the new weapon picked it up and caressed it with four downward strokes of his hand. At each stroke he uttered a different name: Mysterious Weapon, Little Weapon, Weapon That Cries Out, and Possessor of a Good Weapon. These also became sacred names given to the children of the clan.

Then speaking to the messenger, the keeper of the sacred weapon said: "That is the very person for whom we have been in search. Whoever he may be, we shall send him to the abode of

[24]Person, in this usage, means a buffalo bull.

189

spirits." "What course shall we take in approaching that person?" The people asked, and the keeper of the sacred weapon replied: "We will take the path always taken by the sun."[25]

The people approached the person, moving in a westerly direction in imitation of the sun. They made four ceremonial pauses on their way. At the fourth pause the keeper of the sacred weapon lifted the club, brandished it in the air, and the bull suddenly bellowed as though stricken with instant pain. Again the keeper brandished the weapon and the animal started to flee. A third time the keeper brandished the club and the beast was stricken with mortal pain in the hindquarters. At the fourth brandishing of the weapon, the bull whirled around and fell in death, his blood gushing from his mouth.

The people hastened to the fallen animal. They made a slit in the skin, using the sacred knife, that with which they had cut the willow tree, and from the cut fat protruded. As they tasted the fat they said: "It is good; it shall be food for the Little Ones; they shall seethe it in boiling water to prepare it for use." Out of the skin of the left hind leg they cut a round piece, which they called Breast Shield; also two long narrow strips, which they named Red Strap and Strong Strap, which names they subsequently used as personal names. From the skin of the left side on the body they cut seven narrow strips, which they painted red. The straps thus cut they called captive straps, and these served as the original types of straps to be ceremonially made whenever warriors were about to go to war, and to be used by them for tying captives should they succeed in taking any. The round piece of skin called breast shield and which symbolized the sun they also painted red, and it too served as a model for similar shields to be ceremonially made for the warriors and worn by them as symbolic shields as well as charms. At the same time that they made these sacred articles they dedicated the tails, the bladders, and the heart sacs of buffalo bulls to ceremonial use and made them to be sacred types.[26]

[25] When the Osages went to war, they always left the village traveling west. They did this even if the enemy was in some other direction.

[26] La Flesche, *36th Ann. Rpt., op. cit.,* pp. 272-274.

Genesis Myth

(Tsi shu Peacemaker Version)

The Tsi shu were in mid-heaven where the people had acquired souls but they still had no bodies. They wanted to find a place where they could acquire a bodily form and live as persons.

Now the Elder Brothers sent Younger Brother to find a suitable place for them to live. He searched the first of the four upper worlds but found it unsuitable. After searching the second and third upper worlds he rejected them too. In the fourth and lowest of the upper worlds he found the Man of Mysteries.[27] Younger Brother introduced the God to the people saying, "Here is a fear inspiring person, O, Elder Brothers."[28] After the introduction the Man of Mysteries gave the people the names of Little Hawk and Hawk Woman as personal names.

> At this point there is a break in the Tsi shu Peacemaker version of the We ke a as recorded by La Flesche. However, the missing portion was given to La Flesche as a legend and not as a We ke a. We have added the legend here as a paraphrase, in the sequence of the myth.

Younger Brother was sent out to find a way the Little Ones could descend to earth. He found the eagle who gave them wings. Now the people soared toward the earth and alit in a red oak tree.[29] The last two eagles did not have room to light in the red oak. One alit in an alder tree and the other alit amid the Little

[27]Man of Mysteries was a manifestation of Wa kon ta which was also called God of the Clouds and Thunder.

[28]The name No pa walla or Thunder Fear, became a personal name of the Men of Mystery clan. No pa walla refers to the awe inspired by thunder, hence the name is interpreted as Fear Inspiring, Thunder Fear, and Causes Them to be Afraid.

[29]To commemorate the soaring, the Osages wore fringes on their clothing to simulate the fluttering of the wings.

191

Yellow Flowers.[30]

At this point the legend ends.

Now the people met another being, Buffalo Lift Your Head. He threw himself on the earth and the blazing star plant sprang up in all its great beauty. Its taste was bitter, so the buffalo explained it was medicine to keep them healthy.[31] Again the buffalo threw himself upon the earth and the poppy mallow sprang from the soil in its dress of red flowers. This was a medicine, to be used as an astringent. The buffalo instructed the people to make Astringent a personal name.

After this, the buffalo threw himself to the ground and tossed the red corn into the air.[32] Three times more he threw himself to the ground. First, he tossed the blue corn and blue squash into the air. Second, the white corn and white squash. The third time he tossed the speckled corn and the speckled squash into the air. Thus he wedded the corn, a male plant, to the squash, a female plant.

Then the Elder Brothers sent the Younger Brother to make further search. The Younger Brother went to a place where a red oak stood. Under the tree the people gathered and agreed to make the tree a sacred symbol.[33] The brothers moved on until they

[30]Francis La Flesche, "The Osage Tribe: Two Versions of the Child-Naming Rite," *Smithsonian Institution, BAE, 43rd Annual Report,* (U.S. Government Printing Office: Washington, 1928), p. 59; The Little Yellow Flower or cone flower, is a peace symbol of the Tsi shu Peacemaker clan as is the alder branch. Alder branches are comparable to the olive branch of Western Civilization. The eagles that alit in the cone flowers were the Red Eagle sub-clan from which the Tsi shu chiefs were taken.

[31]The Tsi shu Peacemaker clan and Pon ka Peacemaker clan was looked to for medical help.

[32]The red corn differed from the other corn in that it was not accompanied by a squash or pumpkin.

[33]The Tsi shu Peacemaker clan had three red oak acorn personal names. These were Acorn, Profuse, and Profuse Alighting. This group, Tsi shu, alit in the red oak. As they landed, the acorns fell in great profusion. This was taken as a sign that the people would have descendants as numerous as the shower of acorns.

came to a red cedar tree. They made of the cedar a symbol of old age and a long life. Again they moved on and came to the sedge, the grass that never dies, and made of it a life symbol of continuing life. Once more Younger Brother was sent forth. He went to the greatest part of the earth.[34] The Elder Brothers agreed to make the greatest part of the earth a part of their bodies. They took from it the personal names, Mid Earth and Earth.

Now the Younger Brother found a person who lived in a beautiful house.[35] The house had an opening at the top, from this he may have taken a personal name. Now the Elder Brothers also agreed the house was beautiful, and from this they took a personal name, Beautiful House. House Covering was another personal name taken from this person.[36]

The Younger Brother moved on until he came to a bend of a river, there he saw a little house. All the brothers gathered and spoke to the occupant. The occupant was a Hun ka who urged them to accept him as their bodies.[37]

[34]This expression, greatest part of the earth, means the part of summer when the greatness of the earth is shown by ripened fruits.

[35]The House of Peace or Chief's House; Person, as used here, is a personification of the Chief's House.

[36]This refers to the Hun ka house in which children were ceremonially named, the Little House of Mysteries.

[37]La Flesche, *36th Ann. Rpt., op. cit.,* pp. 277-285.

Bibliography

La Flesche, Francis, "The Osage Tribe: Rite of the Chiefs; Sayings of the Ancient Men," *Smithsonian Institution, Bureau of American Ethnology, Thirty-Sixth Annual Report,* Government Printing Office: Washington, 1921.

_____, Francis, "The Osage Tribe: Two Versions of the Child-Naming Rite," *Smithsonian Institution, Bureau of American Ethnology, Forty-Third Annual Report,* U.S. Government Printing Office: Washington, 1928.

CHAPTER X

General Myths

Animal Myths

Buffalo

From the mysterious invisible world, came the buffalo. The adult male and female had full reproductive powers. Birth of the buffalo calf completed the creative act as first the male, then the female and finally the calf emerged into the light of day. They spread over the earth in seven directions, increasing in numbers as they spread.

O pah is used in this myth in two ways. First, it refers to the visible world into which all life comes to live. In addition, it is used to denote the achievement of a desired goal. The coming of the buffalo was for a definite purpose and when the purpose was fulfilled, the buffalo stood as a completed task.[1]

A splinter tribe of the Osage, the Omaha, has a slightly different version than their mother tribe.[2] In the Osage version of the fourth buffalo song the herds arc said to approach from the west, east, south, and north.[3] The Omaha version says they approached from ten different directions and from every direction. Possibly, when the Omaha splintered off they took with them part of the original song. The Omaha personal name, O ke ta, From Every Direction, is not used by the Osages.

[1] Francis La Flesche, "The Osage Tribe: Rite of the Wa Xo Be," *Smithsonian Institution, BAE, 45th Annual Report,* (U.S. Government Printing Office: Washington, 1930), pp. 624-628.

[2] See Omaha version, *Smithsonian Institution, BAE, 27th Annual Report,* p. 293.

[3] La Flesche, *45th Ann. Rpt., op. cit.,* p. 642.

Black Bear

A perfectly made black bear was musing to himself. He felt restless and uneasy as he thought about the four winds. These feelings were the beginning urges which would drive him into hibernation. All at once he stirred into action as he came to some bunch grass. With rapid motions he placed the grass in a pile. The Little Ones observed this act and realized it had a purpose. Black Bear told them if they copied this act they would succeed in war.

Black Bear continued to ponder his hibernation of seven moons. He felt puzzled and lost. Suddenly, he tore up a redbud tree and shredded it into small bits which he placed in a pile. The Little Ones observed this act and realized it had a purpose. Black Bear told them if they copied this act they would succeed in war.

The restless, uneasy feelings still disturbed Black Bear. Now he tore up an arrow-shaft tree and a willow tree. Each time he told the Little Ones they should copy these acts if they wished to be successful in war. Finally, Black Bear tore into a pile of rocks and gathered seven stones for his ceremonial steam bath. If the Little Ones did this they would be victorious over their enemies. Now Black Bear searched until he found a cave. He entered the cave on the right side and slept for six moons. If the Little Ones copied this act they would be successful in war.

When Black Bear awakened from his sleep a moon early he looked at himself. His skin was loose, his toes were folded, his ankles were wrinkled, and his muscles were loose. These were all signs of old age. If the Little Ones made the Black Bear their bodies they would live to see old age.

As Black Bear moved to the right side of the cave entrance he heard the birds singing and smelled the odor of spring. When he stepped outside he left six footprints in the ground. The Little Ones should use these to count their war honors. Now he left seven more footprints and these, too, should be used to count war honors.[4]

[4] Francis La Flesche, "The Osage Tribe: The Rite of Vigil," *Smithsonian Institution, BAE, 39th Annual Report,* (Government Printing Office: Washington, 1925), pp. 154-164.

Beaver

The male beaver was at one end of his house, to the left. He had mud on his face which was to show the Little Ones how to appeal for divine aid when going to war. Now the beaver pushed away from his house making ripples on the water. These were signs of old age like lines on an aged face. When the beaver came to a bend in the river he cut down a yellow willow tree. He said to the people, "This tree represents the people of the west.[5] May you likewise cut down your enemies as you travel the path of life."

After a while he started to drag the tree against the current. In his exertions, he splashed the water with his tail, as Wa kon ta heard the splashing of the beaver's tail, so also, would he hear the prayers of the Little Ones. Beaver then put the trunk of the willow tree to the left side of the entrance to his house.

He then retired to the right side of his house at one end. As he lay resting with moist soil on his face he spoke again to the people. "When you go to war, place soil on your face so Wa kon ta will listen to your pleas and help you overcome your enemies." Beaver then emerged from the left side of his house and again rippled the waters. When he came to a second bend of the river he cut another yellow willow tree. After he had cut the tree, he said, "Many people live toward the setting sun. There are so many that the Little Ones will need this willow to count them."

Again Beaver cut a willow at the third bend and all the other bends until he got to the seventh bend. Here again he cut down a yellow willow. Then he said, "This bend represents the honors of the warrior. They shall use the willow to count their military honors as they travel the path of life."[6]

Another Beaver Myth

There dwelt upon the earth the Wa sha she, who possessed

[5] People of the west is an expression denoting enemies.

[6] La Flesche, *45th Ann. Rpt., op. cit.,* pp. 616-619.

seven sacred fireplaces. None among them were timid or craven.

One of the Wa sha she had made himself a body from the male beaver and stood as a person. The Wa sha she patterned their homes after the beaver house. They took the willow as their sacred tree for it fed the beaver and gave it long life. The beaver went forth against the river current. He noted the ripples and said, "It is the parting of the Water Gods as they make way for me. If the Little Ones make of me their bodies, the Gods of the Waters will make way for them too as they travel the path of life."[7]

Dog

The Little Ones had fallen into bad habits. They could not get along with each other and refused to help each other in times of need. This deeply hurt Wa kon ta so he gave them the dog. The dog was so faithful and helpful to the Little Ones that they once again lived in harmony with each other because they saw the wisdom on these traits.

Eagles

In the Osage myths the golden eagle is considered to be two different species. The immature golden eagle has mottled tail feathers and is called Hu lah Hun ka or Sacred Eagle. Feathers of this eagle are much like the feathers of the European imperial eagle which is not native to America. According to the Osage myths it was the mottled eagle which led the Little Ones from the sky to the earth.

The tail feathers of the mature golden eagle are white with black tips. This bird is called Wa shin ka Wa la hre le ka or The Bird Without Stains. In Osage myths, the mature golden eagle is

---

[7]La Flesche, *39th Ann. Rpt., op. cit.,* pp. 151-154.

not disliked by the other birds. Thus, it is a bird without stains.[8]

Some confusion also exists in references to the red eagle or Hu lah shu tsy. A few writers assume the Osages mistook the red tailed hawk for an eagle. Red eagle refers to the red color of sunrise reflecting from the mottled eagle's back and wings. Thus, red eagle is the symbol of the rising sun. Tsi shu grand division chiefs were always taken from the Red Eagle sub-clan of the Tsi shu Peacemaker clan.

Confusion also exists about the Pa hu scah or White Hair name of the Red Eagle sub-clan. There are at least three different stories about the origin of this name. A popular tale is that it comes from a battle of the French and Indian War. Pa hu scah is said to have scalped a British soldier and got his name from the soldier's white wig. Although this event may be true, it could not be the origin of the White Hair name. This name is a ne ke a or name from the myths of the Tsi shu, therefore, it cannot be a war name. Another story is that the name refers to the white hairs on the top of an aged buffalo's head. This, too, does not seem likely for the Red Eagle sub-clan. Myths of this clan do not mention the aged buffalo but they do mention the white eagle.

The white eagle like the red eagle is symbolic of a time of day and also a time of prayer. Reflected light makes an eagle appear to be white in the midday sun. Around the head this white reflection looks like white hairs. It would seem the name White Hair would refer to this, especially when the connection between the midday sun and the House in the Middle or Chief's House is considered. The white eagle is the symbol of the midday sun.

Avengers

The swallow, the great dragon fly, and the great butterfly are mystic avengers. These three creatures of the air guard the word

[8]Francis La Flesche, "War Ceremonies and Peace Ceremonies of the Osage Indians," *Smithsonian Institution, BAE, Bulletin 101,* (U.S. Government Printing Office: Washington, 1939), p. 205.

of a person. They impose the penalties when a person violates their word or utters a falsehood. Always these guardians of penalities follow people, except in the coldest part of winter. All of these avengers are associated with the rain and thunder. They travel on the wind that rushes in advance of the approaching storms. All possess the power of discernment from which no harmful act can be concealed.[9]

The Owl and Hawk

A leader of a war party, during his seven day fasting time, had a vision. On the first night, the night of strange sounds, the man heard animals in combat and men signaling each other as their footsteps neared and then faded away. After the first night the man was not troubled by animal sounds or the sounds of spirits.

On the sixth night as he lay with his back against a tree, he felt something go past him at a great speed so as to disturb the air near his face. Again the swift passage fanned his face. He lowered his head so he could see what was between him and the faint light of the skyline. Once more the rapid passage and swoosh of air occurred. This time the man saw two birds swoop past. A larger bird was being pursued by a smaller bird. Again they passed, but the smaller bird was being pursued. He heard their cries as they fought and recognized them as an owl and a hawk.

As the morning star appeared in the east, the man again heard the birds approaching. With a sudden dive the hawk landed under the man's bent knees, while the owl swooped on past. The hawk spoke to the man and said, "Protect me against my enemy until the coming of dawn. The darkness of the night places me at a disadvantage. In the pale light of dawn I will defeat my enemy, and I will give you the dauntless courage with which I attack my foes." Now the owl returned, he lit on the ground near the man and angerily spoke, "Give me that person, so I may put him to death. I

[9]La Flesche, *45th Ann. Rpt., op. cit.,* p. 665.

200

also can reward you. You shall have the same power as I possess, to see in the night."

The man moved not, the power to strike his enemy while he slept did not seem courageous to him. His feelings were with the hawk, so he made no move. As the first light of dawn broke over the land, the hawk spoke, "You have granted a great favor, take from my left wing the shortest feather, when you are about to attack attach it to your left shoulder. Then you can do to your enemy what I am about to do to yonder person." The hawk then struck the owl in the head and severed it from the body.

Now the man realized that the power of day is greater than the power of night. Thus, he led the war party, which struck the enemy at dawn and defeated them. The severed heads of the vanquished were placed on stakes as a warning to all enemies of the Little Ones.[10]

Hawk Wa ho pe

The Old Ones, having determined the hawk was suitable for use in a new war ritual as an emblem of courage, began to make a Hawk Shrine, As they were working on the last shrine in the House of Mysteries, they were startled by a sudden clap of thunder. A messenger was sent to see what had made such a great noise. He soon returned and reported Man of Mystery had made the noise. All of the Little Old Men agreed that Man of Mystery was a desirable person, so he was invited to join them and promised the finished shrine would be given to his keeping. With this invitation and promise, Man of Mystery descended and alit on the ridgepole of the House of Mysteries.

Almost immediately there was another terrifying noise outside the door. As the messenger threw aside the door flap there stood a huge enraged buffalo bull. He pawed the earth and

---

[10]La Flesche, *Bull. 101., op. cit.,* pp. 9-11.

bellowed, "I am Buffalo Bull, lift up your heads."[11] Terrified, the Ancient Men threw the sacred emblems toward the angry bull. Seeing this, he at once became quiet and friendly. As a result the Men of Mystery and Buffalo Bull clans are joint owners of the Hawk Wa ho pe or Shrine.[12]

Animals in Great Bodies of Water

The third of the Water Songs speaks in definite terms of the dwelling place of land animals that live in a great lake of the land. Most of the Siouan peoples speak of the presence of both land animals and water animals in large bodies of water. This belief is expressed in the mystic rites and the ordinary myths.

This song makes the following reference to land animals in a great body of water:

"Out of the lake the Great Black One (Bear) shall come.
Out of the lake the Great Panther shall come.
Out of the lake the Sacred Wolf shall come."[13]

Large Animals

Many large animals came from the east. They came up the Osage River to the Pomme Terre River. The animals who occupied the area became angry at the invaders. So terrible was their rage that the Little Ones did not dare to go out and hunt. Thus, they suffered greatly from hunger.

When many of these new large animals and large resident animals gathered on the Pomme Terre River, a terrible battle

[11] This expression means, pay attention. The same meaning is contained in William Shakespeare's, *Julius Caesar*, Act III, Sc. 2, Line 79, "... lend me your ears...."

[12] La Flesche, *39th Ann. Rpt., op. cit.,* pp. 100-101.

[13] La Flesche, *45th Ann. Rpt., op. cit.,* pp. 656-657.

ensued. Many animals on both sides were killed and the survivors resumed their journey toward the setting sun.[14]

In early accounts, the Osages living on the Pomme Terre River were called Big Bone Osages. Osages living on other streams were called Little Bone Osages. The Pomme Terre River was sometimes called the Big Bone River because mastodon and giant ground sloth bones were found there. In all cases the large bones were found where the Osage myth said they would be.

Name Myths

Star Names

The Tsi shu Peacemaker clan gives only four Gods and four Goddesses in their life symbol myths. In the Elder Tsi shu myths, six Gods and four Goddesses are mentioned in the life symbol myths. The list below gives these ten dieties in the order in which they were first met and the order of pairing by sex. The form of address is also included.

(1) Wa kon ta Hum pa to, the God of Day, the sun, term of address, grandfather.
(2) Wa kon ta Hun to, the Goddess of Night, the moon, term of address, grandmother.
(3) Me ka he Hun pa to, the Day Star which is the Morning Star, term of address, grandfather.
(4) Me ka ke Hun to, the Night Star which is the Evening Star, term of address, grandfather.
(5) Wa pa ha, Litter or Big Dipper, Ursa Major or Big Bear, term of address, grandfather.
(6) Me ka ke u ke la sen, Double Star, Theta and Iota in the Orion constellation, term of address, grandmother.

[14]M.F. Ashley Montagu, "An Indian Tradition Relating to the Mastodon," *American Anthropologist,* ns, no. 4, 46:568-571, Oct.-Dec., 1944.

203

(7) Ta pa, Deer Head, Pleiades or Seven Sisters, term of address, grandfather.

(8) Tah la blah, Three Deer, the three big stars in Orion's Belt, term of address, grandmother.

(9) Me ka ke Shu tsy, Red Star, the Pole Star or Polaris, term of of address, grandfather.

(10) Shon ka Ah ka ke a kon, Dog that Lies in the Sky or Sirius, Dog Star, term of address, grandfather.

The Tsi shu Peacemaker and Elder Tsi shu do not give the same gender for the Pleiades or Seven Sisters. The Peacemaker uses a feminine form of address, while the Elder Tsi shu uses a masculine form. The two clans also reverse the gender of Three Deer or Orion's Belt. Controversy over these differences in clan versions are avoided. Each clan gives their rites as they have come down to them.[15]

Sky and Earth Names

(Black Bear and Panther Clans)

Sky names are derived from the myths of creation while the people still lived in the sky. Earth names are also derived from the creation myths, but they come from the time after the people came to the earth.

According to the Black Bear and Panther clans, their first earth names became the names of their clans. The original sky name for the Panther clan was Hun ka Watse ke tse or the Sacred One from the Stars. Hun ka Wa tse ka wa or the Sacred Radiant Star was the sky name of the Black Bear clan. As these two clans traveled over the earth, the Sacred One from the Stars met a Panther and changed the clan's sky name to the earth name of

[15]Francis La Flesche, "The Osage Tribe: Two Versions of the Child-Naming Rite," *Smithsonian Institution, BAE, 43rd Annual Report,* (U.S. Government Printing Office: Washington, 1928), pp. 74-75.

Panther. They next met the Black Bear so The Sacred Radiant Star clan took the earth name of Black Bear.[16]

Earth Names

(Black Bear and Panther People)

The Great White Swan gave the Black Bear and Panther clans three personal names. These are Me ha scah or White Swan; Wa shin ka scah or White Bird; and Moh shon scah or White Feathers. The last name refers to the white feathers strewn on the ground when the swan fell in death.

Earth names given to the Panther clan by a mythical Panther are E gro ka Tun ka or Big Panther, and E gro ka Shin ka or Little Panther, this name can also be interpreted as Young Panther. A mythical Black Bear gave the Black Bear clan the personal names of Wa tse ke tse or He Who came from the Stars; Ki he ka Shin ka or Little Chief; Ki he ka Wa tse or Star Chief; and Wa tse Moie or Traveling Star, a Comet. Sky names that belong to the Black Bear clan are E a scah Walla or He Speaks Clearly which is sometimes interpreted as A Clear Loud Voice. Another sky name of this clan is Pa le Hun ka or Sacred Stranger.

In addition, both of these clans use the earth names of Moh he se e pa blo ka or Round Handled Knife; Moh he Hun ka or Sacred Knife; and Moh he Shu tsy or Red Knife. Nun pa Wa kon ta or Mysterious Hand relates to a mythical power. When the people came from the sky to the earth, they had no weapons. However, they could kill by moistening the right hand index finger with saliva and pointing it at the creature they wished to kill.[17]

[16]*Ibid.*, pp. 48-49.

[17]*Ibid.*, pp. 52-53.

Personal Names

(Buffalo Bull People)

Several personal gentile names are taken from the Songs of the Rising of the Buffalo Bull Men. These are names of the Buffalo Bull clan.

(1) Moh non te ta or He Whose Tread Makes the Earth Rumble, the name describes the noise of a running herd of buffalo.
(2) Sin tse ha la or Tail Curved Back, the name describes the way an angry buffalo bull holds his tail.
(3) Hu gra Tun ka or Big Thighs, a name referring to the great strength in the thighs of a buffalo bull.
(4) Ah pa tu ha or Hump Shoulder, refers to the buffalo hump.
(5) Pa he ka shon or Shakes His Mane, refers to a wounded buffalo bull shaking his mane when brought to bay.
(6) He le tu sha or Curved Horns, refers to the razor sharp hook shaped horns of the young buffalo bull.

The left horn symbolized the knife of a Tsi shu warrior and the right horn the knife of a Hun ka warrior.[18]

Tsi shu Personal Names

As the people were seeking a way to go down to the earth so they could get bodies, the male eagle gave them some personal names. These were Moh shon or Earth; Moh shon ka shon or Travels Above the Earth; and Moh shon U scoh scah or Center of the Earth. Other names arising from this event are He Log ny or Good Eagle Woman; He e ke ta pe or Feathers Fought Over; He ka Moh ka or Feathers Scattered by the Winds; Num pa Se or Yellow Hands; and Wa shin ka He or Feathers of the Bird.[19]

[18]La Flesche, *39th Ann. Rpt., op. cit.,* p. 208.

[19]La Flesche, *43rd Ann. Rpt., op. cit.,* p. 70.

Symbolic Knives

The Black Bear clan was custodian of the four symbolic knives. These knives were called Moh he Se e pa blo ka or Round Handled Knife; Moh he Sop pe or Black Knife; Moh he Hun ka or Sacred Knife; and Moh he Shu tsy or Red Knife.

Sacred knives were assigned to each division, the first two knives were reserved for the Hun ka sub-division. Both the Wa sha she sub-division and the Tsi shu grand division shared the other two knives.

When a warrior used a knife to behead an enemy, the knife he used was considered to be mystically converted to one of the four symbolic knives. Thus, the warrior may count his act as a war honor. In ceremonies, these knives are often alluded to as Wa pa he or Pointed Sharp Weapons.[20]

Special Myths

Upper Worlds

The Osages believed they originated in the lowest of the four upper worlds. At first they had no souls, thoughts, speech, or bodies. They acquired thought in the third upper world and souls in the second upper world. When they ascended to the first upper world they acquired speech. Soon they yearned for bodies. They took the bodies of eagles and soared back down to the fourth upper world which rested on a red oak tree. After they came to earth the red bird gave them human bodies. The Isolated Earth people did not come from the Upper Worlds; they originated on the earth. In the Osage myths, the earth was isolated from the other cosmic bodies.[21]

[20]La Flesche, *39th Ann. Rpt., op. cit.,* p. 346.

[21]Garrick Mallery, "Pictographs of the North American Indians," *Smithsonian Institution, BAE, 4th Annual Report,* (Government Printing Office: Washington, 1886), pp. 85-86.

Tribal Organization

In the beginning the Wa sha she had seven pipes. These were used to keep peace in the tribe. When an argument arose within the tribe, a messenger was sent with a pipe to the disputing parties, and the difficulty was resolved peaceably.

When the Wa sha she met the Hun ka, they were united by the use of one of these pipes. Later, when they met the Isolated Earth people, both groups had pipes of their own, so the Wa sha she and Isolated Earth people exchanged pipes. With this exchange, the Wa sha she, the Hun ka, and the Isolated Earth people became united. At a later time these people met the Tsi shu and also united with them. At this time, the Tsi shu included another sub-division composed of The Men of Mystery and Buffalo Bull clans. This sub-division was called Those Who Were Last to Come.[22]

Formation of the Tribe

In the beginning the Wa sha she, Hun ka, and Tsi shu lived in the Upper Worlds. Eventually, they obtained bodies and souls. Then they descended to earth. After they descended they wandered over the land. The Wa sha she led the way, followed by the Hun ka and lastly the Tsi shu. Many years of wandering brought them to the outskirts of a strange village. As the news was passed back from the Wa sha she to the Hun ka and then to the Tsi shu, the strangers who heard the words, came to see who was there.

Only the Wa sha she entered the village. The Hun ka and Tsi shu refused to enter because they were upset about the condition of the village. Bones of both men and animals were scattered all over the village; a foul odor polluted the air. Men and women conducted themselves in an unbecoming manner. This was a

[22]Alice Fletcher and Francis La Flesche, "The Osage or Wazha' zhe, Tribe," *Smithsonian Institution, BAE, 27th Annual Report,* (Government Printing Office: Washington, 1911), p. 62.

village of death and disorder. The Osages were seeking life and order.

As the leader of the Wa sha she and the leader of the strange people sat down to talk, the Wa sha she leader identified himself as a Hun ka. The stranger raised his hand to his mouth to show his surprise. Then he said, "I am also a Hun ka." The strange Hun ka related how his people destroyed life when it appeared, using the four winds as weapons. Wherever his people directed the winds; all living things fell and died. At this time the Wa sha she invited the strange people to live with them. However, the Wa sha she indicated that his people did not like the habit of destroying life. He further suggested that everyone "move to a new country," where the land was pristine and free of death and disorder. The Hun ka U ta non tse or Isolated Earth as these strange people were called, accepted the invitation and joined the Wa sha she, Hun ka, and Tsi shu.

With the acceptance of the Isolated Earth people a series of changes were made within the tribe. It has been said that shortly after this union, the Wa sha she gave the Hun ka a symbolic pipe. Before accepting the pipe, the Hun ka asked the purpose of the pipe so they would know its use. The Wa she she explained it was a life symbol through which they prayed to Wa kon ta. The Hun ka, in turn, explained the red boulder was their life symbol. It was the symbol of endurance and also a symbol of the sun, the emblem of eternal life. Thus, the Wa sha she and the Hun ka pledged to support each other in times of danger. Since the Isolated Earth people had also united with the Wa sha she, this completed the right side or Hun ka grand division of the tribe.

Another change was to give the Isolated Earth people the Little House of Mysteries. It was here that all the infants were fed the sacred foods of life and given their gentile names in order to have a place within the tribe. The Big House of Mysteries was given to the Black Bear clan and its kindred clan the Panther, both were of the Hun ka division. In this house all ceremonies pertaining to war were held. The four warrior groups, Wa sha she; Hun ka; Tsi shu; and Isolated Earth, conducted the war and hunting actions of the people. No single group could act without including the other three groups. Parties formed under this organization were called the Grand War Party. For many years this arrangement served the people well. Yet, in time, the people grew restless and it became evident that they wished to "move to a new country."[23]

To facilitate the formation of small war parties, greater flexibility was provided in the new reorganization. Little Hawk shrines were introduced to serve in lieu of the old large shrine. Each clan possessed one of these Little Wa ho pe s. Since the hawk was admired for his courage and speed of attack it was a natural choice for a war shrine. It was considered to be a supernatural bird with the sun as its father and the moon as its mother. At times it was called the dark bird or black bird because it was a child of night, the moon.

The myths indicate things did not go well during the reorganization. As the Ancient Men were working on the last Little Shrine they heard a sudden bellow outside. As the flap was thrown aside an angry buffalo was revealed. His head was lowered; his tail was curled and trembling; he was pawing the earth and throwing dust in the air. He announced he was Buffalo Bull. No sooner did he give his name than there was an awesome crash of thunder which shook the earth. "I am Man of Mystery," said the thunder. Speechless with awe the Little Old Men gathered the Little Shrines and threw them toward the Buffalo Bull and Man of Mystery who at once became friendly.

This myth tells us the Buffalo Bull and Men of Mystery clans were upset because of being left out of the reorganization. The act of throwing the Little Shrines toward the bull and thunder, which made them friendly, tells us everything was worked out satisfactorily. Both the Buffalo Bull clan and the Men of Mystery clan were keepers of the Little Shrine. This is the first hint of the

[23]The meaning of this expression is twofold; it is sometimes literal, indicating an actual move to different territory, at other times it indicates a reorganization without a physical move. In both meanings, the change is evolutionary or a gradual change.

presence of these two clans within the tribe, they are called Those Who Were Last to Come. With their addition to the seven Tsi shu clans the Tsi shu division was now complete.

Although the problem of war parties was solved, the people again felt a need to "move to new country." Domestic order had become non-existent. The people were torn by groups seeking vengeance against each other: Disposal of captives often led to disputes among the warriors. No one was safe in their own home. Clearly, some form of civil government was needed. The Little Old Men created the idea of government by two men. They were given the title of Ki he ka or Chief. Two new clans were created to supply these chiefs. Since the chief's function was to preserve the peace, these clans were called Tsi shu Peacemaker and Pon ka Peacemaker.[24]

Hun ka

There was a man among the Hun ka who made of the elk his body. He made a snare of the elk's forehead. Whatever strange beings they may be, or whosoever offspring they may be, none could resist the snare.

Now the Hun ka gathered seven small stones. Four of the stones they placed in the corners of the House of Mysteries. Another stone was a roundhandled flint knife. They made of this stone a personal name for their people. Again Radiant Star, Black Bear, went out and returned with a black flint knife. He went out again and brought back the sacred knife which also became a personal name. Radiant Star went to the far side of a hill and there he found the red flint knife. The Elder Brothers made a personal name of this article too.

Once again the Elder Brothers sent the Younger Brother, Radiant Star, for a needed article. He went to far away lands and

[24]Francis La Flesche, "The Osage Tribe: Rite of the Chiefs; Sayings of the Ancient Men," *Smithsonian Institution, BAE, 36th Annual Report,* (Government Printing Office: Washington, 1921), pp. 60-73.

stood before his Elder Brothers with his bare legs worn with the grasses of the earth. The Elder Brothers asked how things had gone with him. Radiant Star explained that he had traveled to a valley in a far off land, but had found nothing. Three more times Little Brother traveled to as many distant valleys in strange lands.

When he came to the fourth far off valley he beheld the seven bends of a great river, wrapped in a cloud of smoke from many fires. Through the smoke he saw seven villages, one for each bend of the river. He cautiously crept closer so he might observe unseen the people of the villages. Noting the tattoo marks on their foreheads and jaws as well as the closely cut hair of their foreheads, he then slipped away unseen by these strange people.

His manner of approach betrayed his excitement as he reached the outskirts of his village. Noting the excitement of their Younger Brother, the Elder Brothers ran to meet him. Radiant Star related his news as all the Hun ka, Tsi shu, and Wa sha she gathered about him where he stood.[25]

The Tsi shu were not ready for war since they did not have a good supply of weapons. However, the Wa sha she had a good supply of weapons, especially arrows. With the consent of all, the Little Ones went to war with these strange people and eventually defeated them.[26]

The Search for Isolated Earth

In the preparations to enter the House of Mysteries an Osage myth is enacted. The Ancient Men of the Tsi shu gather in a house of their division to prepare. Hun ka Ancient Men gather in a house

[25]This ends the Panther part of the myth. The abrupt ending comes because the conclusion belonged to the He sa ta or Leg Outstretched sub-clan of the Holes in the Wings clan. An eagle leg is attached to the Little Hawk Shrine to commemorate the finding of the foe; it is called Leg Outstretched. The myth concludes with the He sa ta part.

[26]La Flesche, *36th Ann. Rpt., op. cit.,* pp. 201-218.

of their division. Little Old Men of the Men of Mystery and Buffalo Bull clans gather in a separate house of their sub-division.

As the Tsi shu and Hun ka assemble for the ceremonial entry into the House of Mysteries, they pretend to be impatient. Impatience grows as they wait for the Men of Mystery and Buffalo Bull to appear. This wait is symbolic of the long time it took for these two clans to introduce the concept of war parties smaller than one hundred. After many impatient calls the two clans appear, only to stop at the doorway and enter into a debate. In due time, the lagging clans join the procession.

All of this drama preceeding the processional approach to the House of Mysteries refers to a myth. This is the mythical story of the order in which the people marched over the earth when they first descended from the Upper Worlds until they found the Isolated Earth people.[27]

Child's Robe

The Little Old Men often gave the following instructions to a woman who was about to have her first child.

"You are about to have a child. Other children are yet to be born to you. There is in you the same desire that there is in all good mothers to bring your children successfully to maturity. To do this you need the aid of a power greater than humans can give. Secure the skin of an old male buffalo. Dress the skin with your own hands. When it is soft and pliable take some red paint and draw a straight, narrow line from the head, along the length to the tip of the tail. This represents the path of Grandfather the Sun that lives forever. Paint all four legs of the robe red, to represent the dawn, the coming of the God of Day and of life. (See Fig. 8.) Let each child to whom you give birth sleep in the consecrated robe and you will have aid in bringing them to maturity."[28]

[27]La Flesche, *39th Ann. Rpt., op. cit.,* pp. 99-100.

[28]*Ibid.,* p. 194.

Corn Planting

Women had the responsibility of planting corn. The first seven hills had special significance and the grain from these were used in the ceremonies. It was a belief of the Ancient Men that aid from a power greater than human was necessary for a good crop.

On the first day the woman painted a red line down the part of her hair to make a path for all the animals to converge on her. This represented the sun's path and was symbolic of plentiful food, both meat and grain. She must start the planting task as the sun rose on this first day.

Her first task was to prepare seven hills. These were called the Mysterious Hills. In the first hill she planted one grain; in the second two grains. This continued to the seventh hill in which she placed seven grains. If she was from the Hun ka grand division, she patted the dirt over the seed with her right foot. She used her left foot if she was from the Tsi shu grand division. After the first seven hills were planted there were no prescribed procedures.[29]

Striking the Earth

Both the Little Rain Songs and Songs of Striking the Earth describe the joining of Sky and Earth. In the ceremony, the earth was struck with a ceremonial club. The dent was figuratively directly under the midday sun. A vertical connecting the dent and the sun was called Moh go tsa, The Vertical.

In this instance, the dent symbolized the center of the earth and the midday sun symbolized the center of the sky. The earth was struck a second time and the club was used to draw a straight line to the west. Again, the earth was struck and from the dent a wavy line was drawn to the right or south. Once again the earth was struck and a straight line was drawn from the dent to the east. For the last time, the earth was struck and a wavy line was drawn to the left or north.

[29]*Loc. cit.*

By these dramatic actions the Ancient Men gave a description of their concept of the eternal unity of the Sky and the Earth. From this unity, the parade of life marches on into infinity. Additional evidence of this concept lies in the dual organization of the tribe. The Tsi shu grand division represents the sky and the Hun ka grand division represents the earth.[30]

Peace Gods and Goddesses

Although the Old Ones believed in only one Mysterious Life Force, they believed this one Supreme Being took many forms and dwelt in all things. As a convenience of expression, the God and Goddess terms are used to describe the various forms of Wa kon ta. These are not Gods and Goddesses in the old Greek and Roman sense.

Hun pa Wa su was the God of the Cloudless Day. This God was pure and free of the destructive influences of anger, hatred, and revenge. The Tsi shu Peacemaker and Pon ka Peacemaker clans always directed their prayers for peace and good will to this God.

Wa kon ta Hun non pa sa, Goddess of Darkness was also a benevolent diety. She possessed the powers of reproduction. The Little Ones appealed to her for aid in bringing children to maturity. Darkness was perceived as the place of conception. Seeds germinated in the darkness beneath the top layer of soil. Animals are conceived in the darkness of the body cavity or in the darkness of an egg.

Wa kon ta Moh she ta or God of the Upper Regions, like the Goddess of Darkness had the power of reproduction. The people appealed to him to lead them to peace for he was the father who must provide for his children. Life begins with light, the sky is both light and darkness. The God of the Upper Regions was both light and darkness, therefore, he was father to life. The Goddess of Darkness, represented the darkness of both sky and earth,

[30]*Ibid.*, pp. 359-361.

therefore, she was the mother of life.

Wa kon ta Hu tsa ta, the Goddess of the Lower Region or earth, also had the power to bring forth new life. The chiefs and Ah ke ta s prayed to her for aid in the task of leading the people to peace and prosperity. Two mothers is a disconcerting concept to the minds of Western Civilization. To the Osage mind, it was a natural consequence of a reproductive need. The Little Ones believed light and darkness must be wedded, however, they also believed life comes from both the sky and earth, so they must also be wedded. Since the Goddess of Darkness is a child of sky and earth, she represents the mysterious marriage of sky and earth. The Goddess of the Lower Region represents the visible tangible marriage of sky and earth. In a sense, these two Goddesses represented the known and the unknown; belief and knowledge; certainty and uncertainty.

In April, Tah We ta la pe, When the Deer Give Birth to the Young, the two Peacemaker clans conducted a special peace ceremony. This begins a new year since it is the time of new life. The peace Gods and Goddesses are supplicated for aid in providing peace, so there can be a natural increase of the tribe.[31]

Siren

In the Deer Songs a myth of a siren is given. A brother goes hunting for deer and takes his sister with him. She had the power to call the deer so they would come within easy bow shot. The brother shoots a deer, but only wounds it. After a long chase the deer is finally slain and carefully cut up so there is no waste. The song ends with the brother and sister carrying the deer back to their home.[32]

[31]*Ibid.*, p. 147.

[32]*Ibid.*, pp. 130-132.

Mystic Arrows

The Elder Wa sha she clan of the Wa sha she subdivision, conferred upon the Hun ka clan of the Hun ka subdivision the power and authority to organize war parties. A sub clan of the Hun ka clan found the foe, when the tribe as a whole began its warlike career. At that time the Elder Wa sha she offered the Hun ka clan the use of their seven mystic arrows with which to "lay low" the foe. These mystic arrows were pointed with the horn tips of seven deer.[33]

Clouds

Songs of the Clouds were among the most pleasing songs in the Osage rituals. The first two songs speak of the mystery of the clouds rising from the horizon and standing up right. Four of the standing clouds are mentioned as the greatest in mystery.

In the third song, the beauty of the clouds as they vary in color is stressed. The expressions of the people as they look upon the play of colors, adds to the pleasure of this song. Here, the word Mo he or sky is used for cloud, which in normal use is called Moh pe.

Song four shows the awe inspired by the gathering of the colored clouds. The awe grows as the cloud approaches, sweeping along in swift wavy movements.[34]

The Dreams

The youngest of the brothers stood in silent thought. It was spring and the earth was rich in blossoms and ripening fruit. In the evening, he went to one end of the house and fell prone to the earth

[33]*Ibid.*, p. 345.

[34]*Ibid.*, pp. 351-355.

217

with his head inclined to the right and limbs outstretched.

Night passed. The God of Day painted the heavens with pale light. At this, the Younger Brother arose and placed the sacred soil on his brow, then stood motionless. Slowly the God of Day ascended to the zenith, then slid to the edge of darkness. While yet, the sacred soil remained on Younger Brother's brow he wept as he moved to the borders of the village. With his head inclined to the right, he fell prone to the earth and lay outstretched. Wa kon ta made his eyes close in sleep.

Again, night passed. When the God of Day struck the heavens with pale light, Younger Brother arose and again placed the sacred earth upon his brow. He wandered from valley to valley as the God of Day climbed midway in his path. As the God of Day sought to meet darkness, Younger Brother continued to wander. He came to a great gushing spring where he refreshed himself and removed the consecrated earth. Then with his head inclined to the right he fell to the earth where he lay outstretched. Wa kon ta closed his eyes so he could sleep.

The God of Day had not added the sacred colors to his pale colors when Younger Brother arose. He placed the holy soil on his brow and wandered here and there. The God of Day was reaching the Goddess of Night when Younger Brother found a giant elm tree. Even here, within this tree itself, the God of Mysteries may reside. After removing the sacred soil from his brow, he inclined his head to the right and fell to the earth. Wa kon ta caused him to fall asleep.

At the beginning of the next day, Younger Brother again placed Mother Earth upon his brow. He resumed his wandering from place to place. Grandfather passed his zenith and was reaching for the Mysterious Night when Younger Brother came to a low hill. At first, he thought he would spend the night here, but his strength had left him. Fearing his Elder Brothers could not find his body at this place, he strode wearily on, seeking a more accessible place.

After a time he came to a small stream whose banks were covered with scattered groves of trees. Nearby stood a willow, the tree that never dies. Younger Brother fell prone to the earth and though he clung to the willow trunk he could not rise. He then spoke to the willow, "It seems impossible for me to go on, O, grandfather." The tree replied, saying: "O, little one! The people shall always cling to me for support, as they travel the path of life. Behold the base of my trunk which sends out my supporting roots. I have made them to be the sign of old age, O, little one." The willow pointed to his bark, the low outspreading limbs, and the white blossoms of the topmost limbs. These were all signs of old age and long life.

Younger Brother wearily continued homeward. In time, he came to the borders of the village. Here he paused to rest. Then, in a vision, he saw men in deadly combat. Their war clubs were rising and falling in blows and parries. As quickly as it came the vision passed. In his distress, he wondered if it was true that Wa kon ta held young men in special favor. Then, with head inclined to the right he fell asleep. Suddenly he heard a man approaching, treading softly on the earth as he came. Lifting his head, Younger Brother could see no one. After a moment's pause, he again heard a man approaching, the grass swished at his every step. Again Younger Brother lifted his head, but saw nothing.

After a short time, Younger Brother felt another person's foot touch his right foot. Then the stranger spoke: "It is said, a young man is wandering the earth, suffering in body and mind. Is it you?" Younger Brother replied, "Yes, my grandfather, it is I." Then the stranger spoke, saying: "Ha! My Younger Brother, then it is you whose mind is fixed upon the whole earth, with a longing desire. Look upon me!" Younger Brother answered: "O, my grandfather, I look upon you and see every part of your body covered with red." The stranger then said: "Your mind is fixed upon the God whose every part is stained with red. Look upon me again!" In reply Younger Brother said: "I see seven little pipes in your hand. The last one is adorned with scalps of men, O, my grandfather." Again the stranger spoke: "Even upon the sacred pipes your mind is fixed, my Younger Brother. Look upon me again!" The Young man replied: "I look upon you, O, my grandfather, you have a beautiful little portable shrine under your arm." Now, the stranger replied: "Ha! My Younger Brother, your mind is fixed on the sacred shrines. Look upon me again." Then Younger Brother said: "I look upon you, O, grandfather. You stand on seven different kinds of animal skins. They lie softly under your feet." The Stranger spoke, yet, again: "Ha! Younger Brother, you have your mind fixed upon the sacred animal skins. Look at me again!" Now the Younger Brother replied: "As an aged man, I see you, O, grandfather, your face is roughened with the wrinkles of age."[35]

At a first reading this myth may seem to be pointless. Yet, to one who is familiar with the Osage mode of expression, it makes a beautiful point. Younger Brother's dream stranger represents himself and the honors he hopes to attain. It is a story of a youth who finds himself in his dreams.

[35]This is the end of the dreams; La Flesche, *39th Ann. Rpt., op. cit.,* pp. 139-144.

Bibliography

Fletcher, Alice and Francis La Flesche, "The Osage, or Wazha'zhe, Tribe," *Smithsonian Institution, Bureau of American Ethnology, Twenty-Seventh Annual Report,* Government Printing Office: Washington, 1911.

La Flesche, Francis, "The Osage Tribe: Rite of the Chiefs; Sayings of the Ancient Men," *Smithsonian Institution, Bureau of American Ethnology, Thirty-Sixth Annual Report,* Government Printing Office: Washington, 1921.

————, Francis, "The Osage Tribe: The Rite of Vigil," *Smithsonian Institution, Bureau of American Ethnology, Thirty-Ninth Annual Report,* Government Printing Office: Washington, 1925.

————, Francis, "The Osage Tribe: Two Versions of the Child-Naming Rite," *Smithsonian Institution, Bureau of American Ethnology, Forty-Third Annual Report,* U.S. Government Printing Office: Washington, 1928.

————, Francis, "The Osage Tribe: Rite of the Wa Xo' Be," *Smithsonian Institution, Bureau of American Ethnology, Forty-Fifth Annual Report,* U.S. Government Printing Office: Washington, 1930.

————, Francis, "War Ceremony and Peace Ceremony of the Osage Indians," *Smithsonian Institution, Bureau of American Ethnology, Bulletin 101,* U.S. Government Printing Office: Washington, 1939.

Mallery, Garrick, "Pictographs of the North American Indians," *Smithsonian Institution, Bureau of American Ethnology, Fourth Annual Report,* Government Printing Office: Washington, 1886.

Montagu, M.F. Ashley, "An Indian Tradition Relating to the Mastodon," *American Anthropologist,* ns, no. 4, 46:1944, Oct.-Dec.

INDEX

A

absorption of peoples 87
acorns 119
adoption:
    blood 80
    ceremony 85
adornment 47
afternoon songs 55
anise 115
Apache 98
arrowshaft:
    grooves 15
    polishing 114
Arkansas River 98
art, pictorial 155ff
ashes 115
avengers 63

B

bark, use 114
Bartlesville, Oklahoma . . . 99
basic Osage institutions . . . xv
Baxter Springs, Kansas . . . 99
bead drills 169
beads 151
beadwork:
    rosette 166
    rosette design 163
    bonnet 166
    bonnet design 163
    cross 166
    cross design 164

B (cont.)

    evening star 167
    evening star design . . . 165
    girls moccasin 166
    moccasin design 164
    morning star 167
    morning star design . . . 165
    red oak 167
    red oak design 165
    tree of life 167
    tree of life design 165
bear oil 116
beating time 51
bells 151
Biloxi Sioux xi
Bird Creek 99
birth of Hun ka 21
Black Bear:
    clan 180fn
    songs 59
Black Dog I 99
Black Dog Trail 99
black hawk 119
black walnut 116
blackberries 120
blankets 151
bows 102
breech cloth 151
Buck Creek 99
buckeye 116
buffalo hides,
  preserving 105f
buffalo:

B (cont.)

horses. 103
songs 58
trails 98
wallows 106
coming of. . . . . ˙58
rising 59
burial:
adornment 146
changes 147
customs 147

C

caches. 110
Caney, Kansas 99
Caney River 99
captive bands. 47
Catawaba Sioux. xi
catlinite 113
cattail, use 114
Cedarvale, Kansas 98
cedar wind 181fn
ceremonial:
moccasins 44
officials 43
skins 43
charcoal 129
charcoal fight, peace 69
Cherokee 99
Cherokee Outlet 99
Chewere Sioux xi
chiefs. 32f
chiefs:
duties 33ff

C (cont.)

elimination of 35
succession of. 34
child naming 80
child naming ceremony . . . 81
child's robe 83
civil government 32ff
civil-military, separation . . . 35
Claremore, Oklahoma . . . 99
closing the ceremony 65
clothing 151ff
clouds of conduct 22
Coffeyville, Kansas 99
colors:
black 156
blue 156
green 156
Osage. 156
red 156
sources of 172
tints and shades 156
white 156
yellow 156
Comanche 98
coming of humans. 12
coming of the buffalo 19
common law marriage . . . 78
concealing caches. 111
cookery 121
cooking kettles 122
corn:
ceremonies 111
songs 58
uses of. 110
counting:

C (cont.)

stick 5
wands 5
war honors. 57
courtship 74
crop, estimates 109
crow:
belt 57
songs 57
cultural conflicts,
marriage. 79

D

Dakota-Assiniboin
Sioux xi
dangers, hunting 103
Day Star 203
declaring war. 53
decoy 101
Deep Ford. 99
Deer Head. 204
deer song 59
designs, sources of 171f
dewberry root 116
Dhegiha Sioux xi
diamond, design
variations. 159
diamond variations. 158
Director of the Hunt. . . 98,103
division of days 179fn
Dog that Lies in the Sky . . . 204
dogwood bark 116
Double Star. 203
dream prayer. 56

E

early morning song. 49
earrings 151
education, description . . . 88
education, mother's role . . . 93
education, parent's role . . . 92
eight leaders, war 55
Elgin, Kansas 98
Elm Creek. 98
English longbow 103
executive limitation 36
exploring with the mind . . . 10

F

falcata comosa 121
Female Star. 179
fire building. 168
firewood. 117
fish-turtle song. 55
Flint Hills 112
flint, working. 113
footstep prayer 48
Ft. Osage. 99

G

Gibson, Isaac 35
Glasgow, Missouri xiii
God of:
Day 179,203
the Cloudless Day . . . 215
the Upper Regions. . . 215
Goddess of:
Darkness 215

G (cont.)

Night 179,203
the Lower Region.... 216
golden eagle............ 20
good man, defined....... 4
grand buffalo hunt 101
grapes............... 119
graves, looting........ 148
Gravois Mills, Missouri... 99
great evening songs...... 61
great rain songs........ 63

H

hair custom 170
haircuts 15ff
hawk traits 50
head cutters.......... 122
herbs 115ff
Hidatsa Sioux........... xi
hides, deharing 172
ho e ka.............. 157
ho e ka:
variations.......... 158
design variations..... 159
horseback, hunting 102
House of the Little
Old Men.............. 7
Hulah Dam 99
human entities........ 53

I

Independence, Kansas ... 98
Indian Meridian 99

I (cont.)

Indian Turnip 116
isolated hawk song 50

J

judicial powers 36

K

Kansas River xiii
Kaw City, Oklahoma.... 98
kinship terms, children... 81
Kiowa................ 98
Kon za............... xiii

L

La Flesche, Francis,
tribute xvi
language:
body............... 154
dancing 155
dramaturgy 155
oral............... 154
sign............... 155
leader of war party 126f
learning by generations ... 91
life:
after death 9
symbols 177
nature of............. 9
listening courtesy 153
Little:
Earth 181

L (cont.)

Evening Songs 62
Hawk Woman, camp. . . 99
Old Men, defined 3
Rain Songs 63
Rock of the Marsh 16
Yellow Flower 17
loose buffalo hair 106

M

making one strike
  the other 64
making the bow song 53
Male Star 179
Malta Bend, Missouri . . . xiii
Manka Shonka Trail 99
Man of Mysteries 191fn
marriage restrictions 74
maternal uncles,
  in marriage 76
Men of Mystery clan 19
me shin marriage 75
meats, cooking 121
medallions 151
methods of hunting
  buffalo 101
midday sun songs 54
military government:
  final 31
  first 29
  second 30
military tunics 151
milk weed 117
minerals, gathering 112

M (cont.)

Mississippi River xiii
Missouri River xiii
moccasins 152
Monakan Sioux xi
morning star 158f
mourning 143
mourning for fallen
  warriors 144ff
mourning war,
  origin of 143f
mystic powers 39

N

ne ke a 177
Neosho River xiii
Night Star 203
No pa walla 191fn
novaculite 114

O

o me ho marriage 77
O pah 195
opening the shrine 48
organizing a war party . . . 126
ownership of the fields . . . 108

P

papaws 120
parfleche: large design . . . 160
  large 166
  large design 160

P (cont.)

lashing holes 173
small 166
small design 161
making of 170ff
Paw ne no pa she 35
Pawhuska, Oklahoma. . . . 99
Pawnee. 98
Pedee Sioux xi
penalities 66
people of the west 197fn
persimmons 120
persimmons,
  preserving 120
planting 108
Platte River. xi
plums 119
polygamy 73
Pomme Terre
  River xiii,99,202
poppy mallow 115
prayer eagles 20
preserving meat. 105
private hunts 97
processing:
  corn 109
  pumpkins 110

R

Radiant Star. 180fn
Red Star. 204
releasing the arrows . . . 13,64
religion, reluctance
  to speak 39

R (cont.)

Republican Fork. 98
respect toward relatives. . . 170
ribbon work 153
ribbon work:
  description. 166
  designs 162f
rite of vigil 52
right and left 20
rite of vigil 65
rites, divisions of. 39
robes. 152
rush for charcoal, war . . . 60

S

Sacred Leader, war 52
sagittaria latfolia. 121
Salt:
  Creek 98
  Fork 98
  Plains. xiii,98
Sand Creek 99
Sara Sioux xi
Saucy Calf, war
  honors 136ff
seizing firewood 21
selenite. 113
sending the will 67,139
sham:
  attack 70
  name taking. 67
  war, peace ceremony . . . 67
shrines 13
Silver Lake 99

S (cont.)

skinning buffalo........ 104
sky as a head.......... 48
smoking on the skins 43
snake songs 62
snare, the 10
songs, divisions of 41ff
Southern Cheyenne 98
spider 166
spider, design 159
spirit:
  path............. 23,54
  songs 53
standing at his fireplace ... 49
standing clouds 180fn
star songs............. 53
strategies and tactics... 129f
strawberries........... 120
striking the earth... 15,63,166
striking the earth,
  design.............. 159
strouding 153
sumac leaves.......... 117
symbol of eternal sun.... 11
symbolic birth 49
symbolic man 128
symbolism of the rattle ... 51

T

Tails Worn on the Head... 18
taking the rattle song 51
tattooes............... 133
the stand 101
the walkers 132

T (cont.)

third and fourth
  buffalo trails 99
Three Deer 204
tobacco.............. 117
transference of will 9
transmission of myths.... xv
transmission of
  philosophy........... 11
trousers 151

U

unity in thought
  and action 12

V

Verdigris River........ 98

W

wailing songs........... 56
Wa kon ta, defined....... 8
walnuts.............. 119
war:
  adornments 13
  honors 136
  paint 14,129
  party officers........ 127
  with white man....... 36
water chinkapins....... 121
water songs 60
Wa to pa, the 56
Washitas 98
white swan........... 185

W (cont.)

wild bean 121
wild food plants 118ff
wild onions 120
Winnebago Sious xi
winter hunt 107
witch doctors 27
Without Order, discussed . . . 6
wolf:

W (cont.)

songs 50,55
traits 50

Z

zigzag lines 157

****